Say It

Right in

CHINESE

**Easily Pronounced
Language Systems, Inc.**

Clyde Peters, Author

New York   Chicago   San Francisco   Lisbon   London   Madrid   Mexico City
Milan   New Delhi   San Juan   Seoul   Singapore   Sydney   Toronto

The **McGraw·Hill** Companies

Library of Congress Cataloging-in-Publication Data

Say it right in Chinese : the easy way to pronounce correctly / by Easily Pronounce
    Language Systems.
        p.   cm. — (Say it right)
      ISBN 0-07-146919-2
      1. Chinese language—Pronunciation.

    PL1209 .S28   2006
    495.1'152—dc 22   2006049438

    3 4 5 6 7 8 9 10 11 12 13 14 15 16 17 18   LBM/LBM   0 9 8 7 6

ISBN-13: 978-0-07-146919-7
ISBN-10:   0-07-146919-2

Also available:

Dígalo correctamente en inglés (Say It Right in English)
Say It Right in French
Say It Right in German
Say It Right in Italian
Say It Right in Japanese
Say It Right in Spanish

Illustrations: Luc Nisset

Acknowledgments

Betty Chapman, President, EPLS Corporation, www.eplsworld.com
Priscilla Leal Bailey, Senior Series Editor
Xie, Zhen, Chinese Language Consultant
Chen, W. David, Chinese Language Consultant
Chen, Hong, Chinese Character Consultant

This book is printed on acid-free paper.

CONTENTS

INTRODUCTION

The SAY IT RIGHT FOREIGN
LANGUAGE PHRASE BOOK
SERIES has been developed
with the conviction that learning to
speak a foreign language should be fun and easy!

All SAY IT RIGHT phrase books feature the EPLS
Vowel Symbol System, a revolutionary phonetic
system that stresses consistency, clarity, and
above all, simplicity!

Since this unique phonetic system is used in all
SAY IT RIGHT phrase books, you only have to
learn the VOWEL SYMBOL SYSTEM ONCE!

The SAY IT RIGHT series uses the easiest phrases
possible for English speakers to pronounce, and
is designed to reflect how foreign languages are
used by native speakers.

You will be amazed at how confidence in your
pronunciation leads to an eagerness to talk to
other people in their own language.

Whether you want to learn a new language for
travel, education, business, study, or personal
enrichment, SAY IT RIGHT phrase books offer a
simple and effective method of pronunciation and
communication.

PRONUNCIATION GUIDE

Most English speakers are familiar with the Chinese word **Běijīng**. This is how the correct pronunciation is represented in the EPLS Vowel Symbol System.

All Chinese vowel sounds are assigned a specific non-changing symbol. When these symbols are used in conjunction with consonants and read normally, pronunciation of even the most difficult foreign word becomes incredibly EASY!

On the following page are all the EPLS Vowel Symbols used in this book. They are EASY to LEARN since their sounds are familiar. Beneath each symbol are three English words which contain the sound of the symbol.

Practice pronouncing the words under each symbol until you mentally associate the correct vowel sound with the correct symbol. Most symbols are pronounced the way they look!

THE SAME BASIC SYMBOLS ARE USED IN ALL SAY IT RIGHT PHRASE BOOKS!

EPLS VOWEL SYMBOL SYSTEM

(A)
Ace
Bake
Safe

(EE)
See
Feet
Meet

(I)
Ice
Kite
Pie

(O)
Oak
Cold
Sold

(oo)
Cool
Pool
Too

(ĕ)
Men
Red
Bed

(ah)
Mom
Hot
Off

(uh)
Up
Sun
Cup

(Ur)
Hurt
Turn
Her

(ou)
Would
Could
Cook

(ow)
Cow
Now
How

(ew)*
Few
New
Dew

*This symbol represents a sound similar to the French **u**. Put your lips together as if to kiss and say **EE**.

When two symbols appear side by side try to pronounce them as one sound as in the English word "Meow."

TONES

The word **Ma** in Mandarin sounds exactly as in English but has several meanings depending on whether or not the vowel sound rises or falls in pronunciation. The **four** main tones of Mandarin are a **very** important part of the Chinese language and the **EPLS** Vowel Symbol System makes them easy to master!

— **First tone:** A **high** tone reflects a high pitch. The EPLS symbol sits above the syllable to visually illustrate this.

Mother
Mā
M⒜

╱ **Second tone: Rising** tone is reflected in mid to high pitch as in asking "what?" in English. This symbol tilts upward to reflect this tone.

Hemp
Má
M⒜

∨ **Third tone:*** The only tone which goes in two directions. It **starts downward** to the low range then rises. This symbol is placed below the baseline and tilts upwards.

Horse
Mǎ
M⒜

╲ **Fourth tone:** The **falling** tone is similar to saying "Stop!" in a commanding way. The symbol simply tilts downward.

Scold
Mà
M⒜

*There are two very important variations to the third tone as well as a neutral tone. These will be explained on page 3. Have a Chinese-speaking person pronounce some words for you and listen to the variations in sound.

EPLS CONSONANTS

Consonants are letters like **T**, **D**, and **K**. They are easy to recognize and their pronunciation seldom changes. The following pronunciation guide letters represent some unique Chinese consonant sounds.

TS Pronounce these **EPLS** letters like the **ts** in hi**ts** There is a slight puff of air after the **s**. Say wha**t's** **h**appening and try to get a sense of the slight aspiration before the **h**. Very subtle but much appreciated by native Chinese speakers.

DS Pronounce these **EPLS** letters like the **ds** in su**ds**.

ZH Pronounce these **EPLS** letters like **s** in mea**s**ure.

R̲   The Chinese **r** has no exact equivalent in English. You must hear it and try to duplicate the unique sound.

WHAT IS PINYIN? Mandarin Chinese is represented in this book in both Chinese characters and Pīnyīn. Pīnyīn is a romanized phonetic system officially adopted in China. Although Pīnyīn uses many letters that you are familiar with, unfortunately they often vary wildly in actual Chinese pronunciation. Virtually everyone in China can read characters so we have added this feature as an additional tool allowing you to point to what you are trying to communicate.

ICONS USED IN THIS BOOK

KEY WORDS

You will find this icon at the begin-ning of chapters indicating key words relating to chapter content. These are important words to become familiar with.

PHRASEMAKER

The Phrasemaker icon provides the traveler with a choice of phrases that allows the user to make his or her own sentences.

Say It Right in CHINESE

ESSENTIAL WORDS AND PHRASES

Here are some basic words and phrases that will help you express your needs and feelings in **Chinese**.

Hello

Nǐ hǎo! 你好

N_{EE} H_{OW}

How are you?

Nǐ hǎo ma? 你好吗？

N_{EE} H_{OW} M_{ah}

Very good, thanks.

Hen hǎo xièxie. 很好谢谢

H_{uh}N H_{OW} SH_{EE}è SH_{EE}è

Ok / So so

Mǎmǎ Hūhū. 马马虎虎

M_{ah}-M_{ah} H_{oo}-H_{oo}

Literally: Horse Horse Tiger Tiger

And you?

Nǐ ne? 你呢？

N_{EE} N_{uh}

2

Good morning.

Zǎo shàng hǎo.   早上好

DS@ SH@NG H@

Good afternoon.

Xiàwǔ hǎo.   下午好

SH@-W@ H@

Good evening.

Wǎn shàng hǎo.   晚上好

W@N-SH@NG H@

Good night.

Wǎn ān   晚安

W@N-@N

See you later.

Yì hui'er jiàn.   一会儿见

@ H@@R J@@N

Good-bye.

Zài jiàn.   再见

DS@ J@@N

Third tone variations: 1. Notice in the Pīnyīn phrase "Nǐ hǎo" there are two third tones in a row. In actual pronunciation the first tone becomes a **second** or **rising tone**. By following the vowel symbol **which tilts upward** you will do this naturally!

2. A third tone followed by any other tone including a **neutral tone*** becomes a **low tone**. The vowel symbol sits below the base line but does not tilt up. This is by far the easiest tone to master. Just think **low**.

*Neutral tones: A neutral tone means exactly that. You pronounce it with little emphasis and evenly. The EPLS symbol sits on the baseline and **does not tilt** in any direction.

Yes

Shì   是

SH⓾r

Shì almost rhymes with sure but really only has the sh and the r sounds.

No

Bú shì   不是

B⓪⓪   SH⓾r

OK

Hǎo   好

H⓪ⓦ

Please

Qǐng   请

CH⓮NG

Thank you

Xièxie nì   谢谢你

SHⓔⓔⓔ   SHⓔⓔⓔ   Nⓔⓔ

You're welcome

Bú xiè   不谢

B⓪⓪   SHⓔⓔⓔ

I'm sorry

Duìbuqǐ   对不起

D⓪⓪ⓐ-B⓪⓪   CHⓔⓔ

This simple way of saying **I'm sorry** can be used in several situations such as when you want to ask a question or when you are trying to get through a crowd!

I don't understand! (literally: I not understand)

Wǒ bù dǒng.　我不懂

W@h B@@ D@NG

Do you understand?

Nǐ tīng de dǒng ma?　你听的懂吗?

N@ T@NG D@h
D@NG M@h

I'm a tourist.

Wǒ shì yí gè yóu kè.　我是一个游客

W@h-SH@ @-G@ Y@-K@h

I don't understand Chinese.

Wǒ bù dǒng hàn yǔ.　我不懂汉语

W@h B@@ D@NG
H@N Y@

Do you speak English?

Nǐ huì jiǎng yīng yǔ ma?　你会讲英语吗

N@ H@@@ J@@NG
Y@NG Y@@ M@h

Please repeat.

Qǐng nǐ zài shūo yíbìan.　请你再说一遍

CH@NG N@ DS@
SH@@@ @-B@@N

FEELINGS

I would like...

Wǒ xiǎng yào...   我想要

W@h SH(EE)@hNG Y@w...

I want...

Wǒ yào...   我要

W@h Y@w...

I have...

Wǒ yǒu...   我有

W@h Y@...

I know.

Wǒ zhī dào.   我知道

W@h J@r D@w

I don't know.

Wǒ bù zhī dào. 我不知道

W@h B@ J@r D@w

I like it.

Wǒ xǐ huān.   我喜欢

W@h SH(EE) H@@@hN

I don't like it.

Wǒ bù xǐ huān.   我不喜欢

W@h B@ SH(EE) H@@@hN

I'm lost.

Wǒ mí lù le.　我迷路了

Wah MEE-Loo Luh

We are lost.

Wǒ men mílù le.　我们迷路了

Wah-MuhN MEE-Loo Luh

I'm tired.

Wǒ lèi le.　我累了

Wah LA Luh

I'm ill.

Wǒ shēng bìng le.　我生病了

Wah SHuhNG BEENG Luh

I'm hungry.

Wǒ è le.　我饿了

Wah uh Luh

I'm thirsty.

Wǒ kě le.　我渴了

Wah Kou Luh

I'm happy.

Wǒ gāo xìng.　我高兴

Wah Gow SHEENG

INTRODUCTIONS

Use the following phrases when meeting someone for the first time, both privately and in business. Note that **Nín hǎo** is the polite form of hello.

Hello

Ní hǎo   你好   Nín hǎo   您好

N H   NN H

My name is...

Wǒ jiào...   我叫

W J... (your name)

Very nice to meet you.

Hěn gāo xìng jien dao nǐ!   很高兴见到你

HN G-SHNG
JN-D N

GENERAL GUIDELINES

China is the most populous country on earth and is bound by strict rules and courtesy among its people.

- Mianzi (Face) describes shame in Chinese culture. Do not cause shame by insult, embarrassment, yelling, or talking down to a person.

- Guanxi (Relationships) describes the importance placed on having good people-to-people relationships. This is regarded as a sense of personal best as well as a representation of one's influential power.

- Keqi means considerate, polite, and well mannered.

- It is not wise to show public displays of affection, hand waving, and gestures.

NO VERB CONJUGATIONS

The easiest part of learning Chinese is that there are no verb conjugations. **I, you, he, she, it, we**, and **they**, all take the same verb form.

The verb **"to be"** is **shì**. Notice how its form does not change. This holds true for all Chinese verbs!

I am.
Wǒ **shì.**   我是
W@h SH@

We are.
Wǒ mén **shì.**   我们是
W@h-M@N SH@

You are.
Nǐ **shì.**   你是
N@ SH@

You are. (a group)
Nǐ mén **shì.**   你们是
N@-M@N SH@

He/she/it is.
Tā **shì.**   他 / 她 / 它是
T@h SH@

They are.
Tā men **shì.**   他们是 / 她们是 / 它们是
T@h-M@h N SH@

NEGATIVES

A simple way to form a negative in Chinese is to add **bu** (not) in front of the verb.

I eat.	**I don't eat.**
Wǒ chī 我吃	Wǒ **bù** chī 我不吃
W(ah) CH(u)	W(ah) B(oo) CH(u)
I want.	**I don't want.**
Wǒ yào 我要	Wǒ **bù** yào 我不要
W(ah) Y(ow)	W(ah) B(oo) Y(ow)
I understand.	**I don't understand.**
Wǒ dǒng 我懂	Wǒ **bù** dǒng 我不懂
W(ah) D(o)NG	W(ah) B(oo) D(o)NG

A notable execption to the above pattern is the verb **"to have"** which takes the word **méi** before it to say **I don't have**.

I have.	**I don't have.**
Wǒ yǒu. 我有	Wǒ **méi** yǒu. 我没有
W(ah) Y(o)	W(ah) M(a) Y(o)

THE BIG QUESTIONS

Who?

Shuí?   谁？

SH⓪⓪Ⓐ

Who is it?

Tā shì shuí?   他是谁？

TⓐⒽ   SHⒺ   SH⓪⓪Ⓐ

What?

Shénme?   什么？

SHⒺN-MⓊⒽ

What is this?

Zhè shì shénme?   这是什么？

JⒺ   SHⒺ   SHⒺN-MⓊⒽ

When?

Shénme shíhòu?   什么时候？

SHⒺN-MⓊⒽ   SHⓊ-HⓄ

Where?

Náli?   哪里？

NⓐⒽ-LⒺⒺ

Where is...?

...zài nǎ lǐ?   在哪里？

...DSⓘ Nⓐ-Lⓔ

Which?

Nǎ yí gè?   哪一个？

Nⓐ ⓔ Gⓞ

Why?

Wèi shénme?   为什么？

Wⓔ SHⓦN-Mⓤ

How?

Zěnme?   怎么？

DSⓤN Mⓤ

How much? (money)

Duōshǎo qián?   多少 (钱)？

Dⓞⓐ-SHⓞ CHⓔⓔN

How long?

Duō cháng shí jiān?   多长时间？

Dⓞⓐ CHⓐNG SHⓦ JⓔⓔN

ASKING FOR THINGS

The following phrases are valuable for directions, food, help, etc.

I would like...

Wǒ xiǎng yào...   我想要

W@ SH**EE**@NG Y**OW**...

I need...	**Can you...**
Wǒ xū yào... 我需要	Nǐ néng... 你能
W@ SH**OO**-Y**OW**...	N**EE** N@NG...

When asking a question it is polite to say "May I ask" and "Thank you."

May I ask?

Máfán ni?   麻烦你？

M@-F@N N**EE**

Thank you.

Xiè xie ni.   谢谢你

SH**EE**@ SH**EE**@ N**EE**

PHRASEMAKER

Combine **"I would like"** with the following phrases **beneath** it and you will have a good idea how to **ask** for things.

I would like…

Wǒ xiǎngyào... 我想要

W⒜ SH㋪⒜NG-Y⒲…

▶ **coffee**

kāfēi 咖啡

K⒜-F⒜

▶ **some water**

shuǐ 水

SH⒰⒜

▶ **ice water**

bīng shuǐ 冰水

B㋎NG SH⒰⒜

▶ **the menu**

càidān 菜单

TS⒪-D⒜N

PHRASEMAKER

Here are a few sentences you can use when you feel the urge to say **I need**... or **can you**...?

I need…

Wǒ xū yào...　我需要

W**ah** SH**oo** Y**ow**...

▶ **your help**

nǐ bāng máng　你的帮忙

N**EE** B**ah**NG M**ah**NG

▶ **more money**

gèng duō qián　更多钱

G**uh**NG D**O** CH**EE**®N

▶ **change**

língqián　零钱

L**EE**NG-CH**EE**®N

▶ **a doctor**

Yī shēng　方向

®® SH**uh**NG

▶ **a lawyer**

lǜshī　律师

L**ew**-SH**Ur**

PHRASEMAKER

Can you…

Nǐ néng...   你能

N(EE) N(Ŏ)NG...

▸ **help me?**

bāng máng wǒ ma?   帮忙我吗？

B(ah)NG   M(ah)NG   W(ŏ)   M(ah)

▸ **give me?**

gěi wǒ ma?   给我吗？

G(A)   W(ah)   M(ah)

▸ **tell me…?**

gào sù wǒ ma?   告诉我吗？

G(ow)-S(oo)   W(ah)   M(ah)

▸ **take me to…?**

dài wǒ qù...?   带我去？

D(I)   W(ah)   CH(oo)...

ASKING THE WAY

No matter how independent you are, sooner or later you'll probably have to ask for directions.

Where is…?

…zài nǎ lǐ.   在哪里

…DS🖉 N🅐-L🔘

I'm looking for…

Wǒ zài zhǎo…   我在找

W🅐 DS🖉 J🔘

Is it near?

Jìn ma?   近吗？

J🄴N M🅐

Is it far?

Yuǎn ma?   远吗？

Y🔘🅐N M🅐

I'm lost!

Wǒ mí lù le!   我迷路了！

W🅐 M🄴 L🔘 L🅤

PHRASEMAKER

▶ **Restroom...**

Xǐ shǒu jiān...   洗手间

SH🖾 SH🔘 J🖾🖾N...

▶ **Telephone...**

Diànhuà...   电话

D🖾🖾N H🔘🔘🔘...

▶ **Beach...**

Hǎitān...   海滩

H🅘 T🅐N...

▶ **Hotel..**

Lǚguǎn...   旅馆

L🅔🅦 G🔘🔘🅐N...

▶ **The train for...**

Huǒ chē...   火车

H🔘🔘🅐 CH🔘🔘...

...where is it?

...zài nǎ lǐ.   在哪里

...DS🅐 N🅐-L🖾

TIME

What time is it?

Xiànzài jǐdiǎn?   现在几点？

SHEEÊN DSÒ JEE DEEÊN

Morning

Zǎoshàng   早上

DSow SHÆNG

Noon

Zhōngwǔ   中午

JÔNG Woo

Night

Wǎnshàn   晚上

Wah)N SHÆN

Today

Jīntiān   今天

JEEN TEEÊN

Tomorrow

Míngtiān   明天

MÆNG TEEÊN

This week

Zhè gè xīngqī   这个星期

J⑩ G⑩ SH⑩NG CH⑩

This month

Zhè gè yuè   这个月

J⑩ G⑩ Y⑩⑩

This year

Jīn nián   今年

J⑩N N⑩⑩N

Now

Xiàn zài   现在

SH⑩⑩N DS⑩

Soon

Hěn kuài   很快

H⑩N K⑩⑩

Later

Yì huǐ 'er   一会儿

⑩ H⑩⑩⑩R

Never

Cóng lái bú huì   从来不会

TS⑩NG L⑩ B⑩ ⑩⑩⑩

WHO IS IT?

I

Wǒ   我

W@h

You

Nǐ   你

N@@

He / she / it

Tā   他（她，它）

T@h

We

Wǒ mén   我们

W@h-M@@N

You (plural)

Nǐ mén   你们

N@@-M@@N

They

Tā men   他们（她们，它们）

T@h-M@@N

THIS AND THAT

The equivalents of **this, that, these,** and **which** are as follows:

This

Zhè   这

J@

This is mine.

Zhè shì wǒde   这是我的

J@ SH@ W@-D@

That

Nà   那

N@

That is mine.

Nà shì wǒde.   那是我的

N@ SH@ W@-D@

These

Zhè xiē   这些

J@ SH@@

These are mine.

Zhè xiē shì wǒde.   这些是我的

J@ SH@@ SH@ W@-D@

USEFUL OPPOSITES

Near

Jìn   近

J®N

Far

Yuǎn   远

Y⊚@N

Here

Zhè li   这里

J@-L®

There

Nà li   那里

N@-L®

Left

Zuǒ biān   左边

DS⊚@-B®®N

Right

Yòu biān   右边

Y∅-B®®N

A little

Yì diǎn   一点

® D®®N

A lot

Hěn duō   很多

H@N D⊚@

More

Gèng duō   更多

G@NG D⊚@

Less

Gèng shǎo   更少

G@NG SH⊚

Big

Dà   大

D@

Small

Xiǎo   小

SH®⊚

Open	Closed
Kāi 开	Guān 关
K①	G⑩ⓐⓗN

Cheap	Expensive
Pián yì 便宜	Guì 贵
PⒺⒺⓇN ⒺⒺ	G⑩Ⓐ

Clean	Dirty
Gān jìng 干净	Zāng 脏
GⓐⓗN JⒺNG	DSⓐⓗNG

Good	Bad
Hǎo 好	Huài 坏
HⓄⓌ	H⑩Ⓘ

Vacant	Occupied
Méi rén yòng 没人用	Yǒu rén yòng 有人用
MⒶ RⓊN YONG	Y① RⓊN YONG

Right	Wrong
duì 对	cuò 错
D⑩Ⓐ	TS⑩ⓐⓗ

WORDS OF ENDEARMENT

I like you.

Wǒ xǐ huān nǐ.   我喜欢你

W⒜ SH㊗ H⑳⒜N N㊙

I love you.

Wǒ ài nǐ.   我爱你

W⒜ ⊘ N㊙

I love China.

Wǒ ài zhōngguó.   我爱中国

W⒜ ⊘ J⓪NG-G⑳⒜

I love Beijing.

Wǒ ài běijīng.   我爱北京

W⒜ ⊘ BⒶ-J㊙NG

I love Shanghai.

Wǒ ài shànghǎi.   我爱上海

W⒜ ⊘ SH⒜NG-H①

I love Hong Kong.

Wǒ ài xiānggǎng.   我爱香港

W⒜ ⊘ SH㊙⒜NG G⒜NG

WORDS OF ANGER

Go away!

Zǒu kāi!   走开！

DS◎ K①

Stop bothering me!

Bié fán wǒ!   别烦我！

Bⓔⓔⓔ Fⓐⓝ Wⓐⓝ

What do you want?

Nǐ xiǎng gàn shéngme?   你想干什么？

Nⓔⓔ SHⓔⓔⓐⓝNG GⓐⓝN SHⓐⓝNG-Mⓤⓗ

Be quiet!

Ān jìng!   安静！

ⓐⓗN JⓔⓔNG

That's enough!

Gòu lé!   够了！

G◎ Lⓤⓗ

COMMON EXPRESSIONS

When you are at a loss for words but have the feeling you should say something, try one of these!

No problem.

Méi wèntí!   没问题

M○A W○○N-T○E

Congratulations!

Gong xǐ!   恭喜

G○○NG SH○E

Good fortune!

Gong xǐ fācái!   恭喜发财

G○○NG SH○E F○ah-TS○

Welcome!

Huānyíng!   欢迎

H○○○ahN-Y○ENG

Cheers!

Gān bēi!   干杯！

G○ahN B○A

Good luck!

Zhù nǐ hǎo yùn!　祝你好运

JOO NEE HOW YOON

My goodness!

Tiān a!　天啊！

TEEĕN ah

What a shame! / That's too bad.

Hěn zāo gāo.　很糟糕

HuhN DSOW GOW

Wonderful! Fantastic!

Tài hǎo le!　太好了

TȲ HOW Luh

USEFUL COMMANDS

Stop!

Tíng! 停

T**ⓔ**NG

Go!

Zǒu ba! 走吧！

DS**ⓞ** B**ⓐh**

Wait!

Děng yí xià! 等一下！

D**ⓤh**NG **ⓔ** SH**ⓔⓔⓐh**

Hurry!

Kuài diǎn! 快点

K**ⓞⓞ** D**ⓔⓔⓔ**N

Slow down!

Màn diǎn! 慢点！

M**ⓐⓗ**N D**ⓔⓔⓔ**N

Come here!

Dào zhè lái! 到这来！

D**ⓞⓦ** J**ⓤ** L**ⓘ**

EMERGENCIES

Fire!

Zháo huǒ le!   着火了!

JOW HOO@n LWh

Help!

Jiù mìng!   救命!

J@@NG M@NG

Emergency!

Jǐn jí qíng kuàng!   紧急情况!

J@N-J@ CH@NG K@@NG

Call the police!

Jiào jǐng chá!   叫警察!

J@@W J@NG-CH@n

Call a doctor!

Jiào yī shēng!   叫医生!

J@@W @ SH@NG

Call an ambulance!

Jiào jiù hù chē!   叫救护车!

J@@W J@@ H@-CH@

ARRIVAL

Passing through customs should be easy since there are usually agents available who speak English. You may be asked how long you intend to stay and if you have anything to declare.

- Have your passport ready.

- Be sure all documents are up-to-date.

- Chinese law is strict and items such as videotaping equipment or movie cameras should be declared upon entry.

- Time used throughout China is Beijing standard time, which is thirteen hours ahead of New York.

- While in a foreign country, it is wise to keep receipts for everything you buy.

- Be aware that many countries will charge a departure tax when you leave. Your travel agent should be able to find out if this affects you.

- If you have connecting flights, be sure to reconfirm them in advance.

- Make sure your luggage is clearly marked inside and out and always keep an eye on it when in public places.

- Take valuables and medicines in carry-on bags.

KEY WORDS

Baggage

Xínglǐ 行李

SH**ⓔ**NG L**ⓔⓔ**

Customs

Hǎi guān 海关

H**ⓘ** G**ⓞⓞⓐⓗ**N

Documents

Wén jiàn 文件

W**ⓦ**N J**ⓔⓔ ⓔ**N

Passport

Hù zhào 护照

H**ⓞⓞ** J**ⓞⓦ**

Porter

Bān yùn gōng 搬运工

B**ⓐⓗ**N Y**ⓞⓞ**N G**ⓞ**NG

Tax

Shuì 税

SH**ⓞⓞⓔ**

USEFUL PHRASES

Here is my passport.

Zhè shì wǒ de hù zhào.　这是我的护照

J⒰　SH⒰　W⒜h　D⒰h
H⒪⒪　J⒪w

I have nothing to declare.

Wǒ méi yǒu dōng xī yào shēn bào.
我没有东西要申报

W⒜h　M⒠-Y⒪　D⒪NG-SH⒠
Y⒪w　SH⒰hN-B⒪w

I'm here on business.

Wǒ shì lái tán shēng yì de.　我是来谈生意的

W⒜h　SH⒰　L⒤
T⒜N-SH⒰hNG-⒠　D⒰h

I'm on vacation.

Wǒ zài dù jià.　我在度假

W⒜h　DS⒤　D⒪⒪-J⒠⒜h

Is there a problem?

Yǒu wèn tí ma?　有问题吗？

Y⒪　W⒰hN-T⒠　M⒜h

PHRASEMAKER

I'll be staying...

Wǒ yào zhù...   我要住

W(ah) Y(ow) J(oo)...

▸ **one night**

yígè wǎnshàng   一个晚上

(EE)-G(uh) W(ah)N-SH(ah)NG

▸ **two nights**

liǎng gè wǎn shàng   两个晚上

L(EE)(ah)NG-G(uh) W(ah)N-SH(ah)NG

▸ **one week**

yígè xīngqī   一个星期

(EE)-G(uh) SH(EE)NG-CH(EE)

▸ **two weeks**

liǎnggè xīngqī   两个星期

L(EE)(ah)NG-G(uh) SH(EE)NG-CH(EE)

USEFUL PHRASES

I need a porter.

Wǒ yào yí gè bān yùn gōng.　我要一个搬运工

Wah Yow EE-Guh
BahN-YOoN-GOoNG

These are my bags.

Zhè xiē shì wǒ de bāo.　这些是我的包

ZHuh SHEE-eh SHuh
Wah Duh Bow

I'm missing a bag.

Wǒ diù le yí gè bāo.　我丢了一个包

Wah DEEOo Luh
EE-Guh Bow

Thank you. This is for you.

Xiè xie. Zhè shì gěi nǐ de.　谢谢。这是给你的。

SHEE-eh SHEE-eh
Juh SHuh GA NEE Duh

PHRASEMAKER

To say **Where is...?**, name
what you are looking for then
go to bottom of the page and say...**zài nǎ lǐ?**

▶ **Customs...**

Hǎi guān... 海关

H**①** G**⓪⓪ⓐⓗ**N...

▶ **Baggage claim...**

Rèn lǐng xíng lǐ... 认领行李

B**⓪**N L**ⓔⓔ**NG SH**ⓔ**NG L**ⓔⓔ**...

▶ **The money exchange...**

Yài-bì dùi huàn... 外币兑换

Y**①** B**ⓔⓔ** D**⓪⓪Ⓐ** H**⓪⓪ⓐ**N...

▶ **The taxi stand...**

Chū zū chē... 出租车

CH**⓪⓪** DS**⓪⓪** CH**ⓤⓗ**...

▶ **The bus stop...**

Gōng gòng qì chē zhàn... 公共汽车站

G**⓪**NG-G**⓪**NG CH**ⓔ** CH**ⓤⓗ** J**ⓐ**N...

...where is?

...zài nǎ lǐ? 在哪里？

...DS**①** N**ⓐ**-L**ⓔⓔ**

HOTEL SURVIVAL

A wide selection of accommodations is available in major cities. The most complete range of facilities is found in five star hotels.

- Make reservations well in advance and request the address of the hotel to be written in Chinese as most taxi drivers do not speak English.

- Faxing is the best way to make your reservations and is customary in China.

- Do not leave valuables or cash in your room when you are not there!

- Electrical items like blow-dryers may need an adapter and/or connector. Your hotel may be able to provide one, but to be safe, take one with you.

- It is a good idea to make sure you give your room number to persons you expect to call you. This can avoid confusion with western names.

- Your hotel front desk can usually assist you with posting mail or packages and many tourist hotels have their own post offices and shipping services.

KEY WORDS

Hotel

Lǚ guǎn 旅馆

L

Bellman

Xíng lǐ yuán 行李员

SHENG LEE YOOAN

Maid

Fú wù yuán 服务员

FOO WOO YOOAN

Message

Duǎn xìn 短信

DOOAN SHEN

Reservation

Yù dìng 预定

YOO DENG

Room service

Kè fáng fú wù 客房服务

KE FONG FOO WOO

CHECKING IN

My name is…

Wǒ jiào...   我叫

Wah Jⓔⓔⓞⓦ…

I have a reservation.

Wǒ yǐ jīng yù dìng le.   我已经预定了

Wⓐⓗ-ⓔⓔ JⓔⓔNG
Yⓞⓞ DⓔNG Lⓤⓗ

Have you any vacancies?

Yǒu méi yǒu kòng fáng?   有没有空房？

Yⓞ Mⓐ Yⓞ
KⓞNG FⓐNG

What is the charge per night?

Fáng fèi yì tiān dōu shǎo qián?   房费一天多少钱？

FⓐNG Fⓐ ⓔⓔ
TⓔⓔⓔN Dⓞ SHⓞⓦ CHⓔⓔⓔN

Is there room service?

Yǒu meí yǒu kè fáng fú wù?   有没有客房服务？

Yⓞ Mⓐ Yⓞ
Kⓞⓤ FⓐNG Fⓞⓞ Wⓞⓞ

PHRASEMAKER

I would like a room with...

Wǒ xiǎng yào yǒu ...　我想要有

W**ⓐ** SH**Ⓔ**ⓐNG Y**ⓞⓦ** Y**ⓞ**...

▸ **a bath**

xǐ shǒu jiān de fángjiān　洗手间 的房间

SH**Ⓔ** SH**ⓞ** J**Ⓔ**ⓔN
D**ⓤⓗ** F**ⓐ**NG J**Ⓔ**ⓔN

▸ **one bed**

yì jìan wò shì de fángjiān　一间卧室 的房间

Ⓔ J**Ⓔ**ⓔN W**ⓐ** SH**ⓤ**
D**ⓤⓗ** F**ⓐ**NG J**Ⓔ**ⓔN

▸ **two beds**

liǎng jiān wò shì de fángjiān
两间卧室 的房间

L**Ⓔ**ⓐNG J**Ⓔ**ⓔN W**ⓐ** SH**ⓤ**
D**ⓤⓗ** F**ⓐ**NG J**Ⓔ**ⓔN

▸ **a shower**

yù shì de fángjiān　浴室 的房间

Y**ⓞⓞ** SH**ⓤ**
D**ⓤⓗ** F**ⓐ**NG J**Ⓔ**ⓔN

USEFUL PHRASES

My room key, please.

Qǐng gěi wǒ fáng jiān yào shì.　请给我房间钥匙

CH**E**NG G**A**
W**ah** F**A**NG J**EE**ⓔN
Y**ow** SH**U**

Are there any messages for me?

Yǒu méi yǒu gěi wǒ de liú yán?　有没有给我的留言？

Y**O** M**A** Y**O**
G**A** W**ah** D**uh** L**EE**ⓞ Y**ah**N

Where is the dining room?

Cān tīng zài nǎ lǐ?　餐厅在哪里？

TS**ah**N T**EE**NG DS**I** N**ah** L**EE**

Are meals included?

Bāo kuò cān fèi ma?　包括餐费吗？

B**ow** K**oo**ⓐ
TS**ah**N F**A** M**ah**

What time is breakfast?

Shénme shíhòu yǒu zǎo cān?　什么时候有早餐？

SH**ⓐ**N-M**uh** SH**oo**-H**O**
Y**O** DS**ow** 1S**ah**N

PHRASEMAKER
(WAKE UP CALL)

Please wake me at...

Qǐng jiào xǐng wǒ...　请叫醒我

CH**EE**NG J**EE**⊚ SH**E**NG W**ah**...

▶ **6:00 a.m.**

zǎo chén liù diǎn　早晨六点

DS⊚ CH**U**N L**EE**⊚ D**EE**⊛N

▶ **6:30 a.m.**

zǎo chén liù diǎn bàn　早晨六点半

DS⊚ CH**U**N L**EE**⊚ D**EE**⊛N B**ah**N

▶ **7:00 a.m.**

zǎo chén qī diǎn　早晨七点

DS⊚ CH**U**N CH**EE** D**EE**⊛N

▶ **7:30 a.m.**

zǎo chén qī diǎn bàn　早晨七点半

DS⊚ CH**U**N CH**EE** D**EE**⊛N B**ah**N

▶ **8:00 a.m.**

zǎo chén bā diǎn　早晨八点

DS⊚ CH**U**N B**ah** D**EE**⊛N

▶ **9:00 a.m.**

zǎo chén jǔ diǎn　早晨九点

DS⊚ CH**U**N J⊚ D**EE**⊛N

PHRASEMAKER

I need…

Wǒ xūyào...   我需要

W@h SH⊚⊚-Y⊚w...

▶ **a babysitter**

bǎo mǔ   保姆

B⊚w M⊚⊚

▶ **a bellman**

xíng lǐ yuán   行李员

SH@NG L@ Y⊚⊚@N

▶ **more blankets**

gèng duō máo tǎn   更多毛毯

G@NG D⊚⊚@h M⊚w T@N

▶ **a hotel safe**

bǎo xiǎn xiāng   保险箱

B⊚w SH@@@N SH@@@NG

▶ **ice cubes**

bīng kuài   冰块

B@NG K⊚⊚⦸

▶ **an extra key**

lìng wài yì bǎ yàoshi 另外一把钥匙

LEENG-WI EE Bah
YOW-SHUr

▶ **a maid**

fú wù yuán 服务员

FOO WOO YOOaN

▶ **the manager**

jīng lǐ 经理

JEENG LEE

▶ **clean sheets**

gān jìng de chuáng dān 干净的床单

GahN JEENG Duh
CHOOaNG DahN

▶ **soap**

féi zào 肥皂

FA DSOw

▶ **toilet paper**

wèi shēng zhǐ 卫生纸

WA SHuhNG JUS

▶ **more towels**

gèng duó máo jīn 更多毛巾

GuNG DOOaw MOw JEEN

PHRASEMAKER

(PROBLEMS)

There is no…

Méi yǒu...   没有

M⒜ Y◎...

▸ **electricity**

diàn le   电了

D㋒⒪N L⒰

▸ **heat**

nuǎng qì le   暖气了

N⒪⒜NG CH㋒ L⒰

▸ **hot water**

rè shuǐ le   热水了

R⒲ SH⒪⒜ L⒰

▸ **light**

dēng le   灯了

D⒲NG L⒰

▸ **toilet paper**

wèi shēng zhǐ le   卫生纸了

W⒜ SH⒲NG J⒰ L⒰

PHRASEMAKER

(SPECIAL NEEDS)

Do you have...

Nǐ zhè'er yǒu...   你这有

NEE JOOB YO...

▶ **an elevator?**

diàn tī ma?   电梯吗?

DEEON TEE Mah

▶ **a ramp?**

xié pō dào ma?   斜坡道吗?

SHEE PO DOW Mah

▶ **a wheel chair?**

lún yǐ ma?   轮椅吗?

LOON EE Mah

▶ **facilities for the disabled?**

cánjí rén shè shī ma?   残疾人用具吗?

TSaN-JEE BOON
SHOO SHUr Mah

CHECKING OUT

The bill, please.

Qǐng gěi wǒ zhàng dān.   请给我账单

CH⊛NG G⊛ W⊛
J⊛NG D⊛N

Is this bill correct?

Zhè gè zhàng dān duì ma?   这个账单对吗？

J⊛ G⊛ J⊛NG
D⊛N D⊚⊛ M⊛

Do you accept credit cards?

Kéyǐ yòng xìnyòng kǎ ma?   可以用信用卡吗？

K⊛-Y⊛ Y⊘NG
SH⊛N-Y⊘NG K⊛ M⊛

Could you have my luggage brought down?

Néng bāng wǒ bǎ xínglǐ ná xià lái ma?
能帮我把行李拿下来吗？

N⊛NG B⊛NG
W⊛ B⊛ SH⊛NG-L⊛
N⊛ SH⊛⊛ L⊘ M⊛

Please call a taxi.

Qǐng jiào chūzūchē.   请叫出租车

CH**ⓔ**NG J**ⓔ**ⓞⓦ
CH**ⓞⓞ**-DS**ⓞⓞ**-CH**ⓤⓗ**

I had a very good time!

Wǒ zài zhè lǐ guò de hěn yú kuài.   我在这里过得很愉快

W**ⓐⓗ** DS**ⓘ** J**ⓤⓗ**
L**ⓔ** G**ⓞⓞ**ⓐⓗ D**ⓤⓗ**
H**ⓤⓗ**N Y**ⓞⓞ** K**ⓞ**ⓘ

Thanks for everything.

Xiè xie wèi wǒ zuò de yí qiè.   谢谢为我做的一切

SH**ⓔ**ⓔ**ⓔ** SH**ⓔ**ⓔ**ⓔ**
W**ⓘ** W**ⓐⓗ** DS**ⓞⓞ**ⓐⓗ
D**ⓤⓗ** **ⓔⓔ** CH**ⓔ**ⓔ**ⓔ**

We'll see you next time.

Wǒ men xià cì zài jiàn.   我们下次再见

W**ⓐⓗ**-M**ⓤⓗ**N SH**ⓔ**ⓔ**ⓐⓗ**
TS**ⓤ** DS**ⓘ** J**ⓔ**ⓔ**ⓔ**N

Good-bye

Zài jiàn   再见

DS**ⓘ** J**ⓔ**ⓔ**ⓔ**N

RESTAURANT SURVIVAL

China boasts one of the world's greatest cuisines and enjoys high marks for color, flavor, and aroma. Chinese food is very popular and you will find a variety of specialties. that are both delicious and inexpensive

- Beijing breakfast snacks sold by street vendors are worth trying. They consist of vegetables wrapped in an omelette wrapped in a pancake and are called **Jiān bǐng.**

- In many cases some of the least expensive restaurants serve up the tastiest dishes.

- You will not find traditional Chinese meals in western fast-food restaurants.

- Ordering foods is a joint affair and the dishes are served and placed in the center of table for all to enjoy.

- Mineral water in plastic bottles is available in most cities as tap water is not suitable for drinking.

- It is the customary for one person to pay the bill as splitting a bill is not done.

- There are no taxes or tipping.

KEY WORDS

Breakfast

Zǎo cān 早餐

DS🄐 TS🄐N

Lunch

Wǔ cān 午餐

W🄐 TS🄐N

Dinner

Wǎn cān 晚餐

W🄐N TS🄐N

Waiter

Fú wù yuán 服务员

F🄐 W🄐 Y🄐🄐N

Waitress

Fú wù yuán 服务员

F🄐 W🄐 Y🄐🄐N

Restaurant

Fàn diàn 饭店

F🄐N D🄐🄐N

USEFUL PHRASES

The menu, please.

Qǐng gěi wǒ cài dān.　请给我菜单

CHENG GA Wah
TSO DahN

Separate checks, please.

Fēn kāi fù zhàng.　分开付帐

FuhN KI Foo JahNG

We are in a hurry.

Wǒ men yǒu jí shì.　我们有急事

Wah-MuhN YO JEE SHur

What do you recommend?

Nǐ yǒu shénme kěyǐ tuī jiàn dēma?
你有什么可以推荐的吗？

NEE YO SHuhN-Muh
Kuh-YEE TooA
JEEuhN Duh-Mah

Please bring me...

Qǐng gěi wǒ...   请给我

CH**ⓔ**NG G**Ⓐ** W**ⓐ**...

Please bring us...

Qǐng gěi wǒmen...   请给我们

CH**ⓔ**NG G**Ⓐ** W**ⓐ**-M**ⓤ**N

I'm hungry.

Wǒ è le.   我饿了

W**ⓐ** **ⓤ** L**ⓤ**

I'm thirsty.

Wǒ kě le.   我渴了

W**ⓐ** K**ⓤ** L**ⓤ**

Is service included?

Bāokùo fúwùfèi ma?   包括服务费吗？

B**ⓞⓦ**-K**ⓞⓞⓐ** F**ⓞⓞ** W**ⓞⓞ** F**Ⓐ** M**ⓐ**

The bill, please.

Qǐng gěi wǒ zhàng dǎn.   请给我账单

CH**ⓔ**NG G**Ⓐ**

W**ⓐ** J**ⓐⓩ**NG D**ⓐⓗ**N

CHINESE CUISINES AND STYLES

The remainder of this chapter will help you order foods you are familiar with. On these pages you will find information on "Dish Systems," customs, and utensils commonly used in China.

Utensils:

Chopstick are used as tableware in China and are considered to reflect gentleness rather than the knife and fork used in Western civilization.

It is not a good idea to place chopsticks upright in your rice bowl as it is observed as impolite.

Dish Styles:

There are eight "Dish Systems" in China. Each dish system stresses a variety of cooking combinations and entrees with respective oils, sauces, spiciness, tenderness, and crispness features.

Famous Dish Systems:

Three famous cuisines in Chinese cooking are Sichuan, Shandong, and Guangdon (Cantonese) dishes. They vary from Sichuan Dish (hot and tangy) to the Shandong Dish (fresh, crisp, and light).

One very popular dish is Beijing Roast Duck. As with other dishes from the Beijing area, it has its roots in many hundreds of years of Chinese cooking. This delectable dish is one not to be missed!

Cantonese cuisine is one of the four main cuisines in China and encompasses crisp, tender and quick-fried dishes, such as Shark's Fin and Bird's Nest.

Beverage:

Tea (cha) is the most popular drink in China. Make sure the spout is facing out from the table.

BEVERAGE LIST

Coffee
Kā fēi   咖啡

K⒜-F⒜

Decaffeinated coffee
Wú kā fēi yīn kā fēi   无咖啡因咖啡

W⓪ K⒜-F⒜ ⒠N K⒜-F⒜

Tea
Chá   茶

CH⒜

Cream
Jiā nǎi de   加奶的

J⒠⒜ N① D⒰

Sugar
Jiā táng de   加糖的

J⒠⒜ T⒜NG D⒰

Ice
Jiā bīng de   加冰的

J⒠⒜ B⒠NG D⒰

Lemon
Jiā níng méng de   加柠檬的

J⒠⒜ N⒠NG M⒪NG D⒰

Milk

Níu nǎi   牛奶

NEEoo NⓍ

Hot chocolate

Rè qiǎo kē lì   热巧克力

Burr CHEEow Kuh LEE

Juice

Guǒ zhī   果汁

GOOah JUr

Orange juice

Chéng zhī   橙汁

CHWNG JUr

Ice water

Bīng shuǐ   冰水

BEENG SHOOA

Mineral water

Kuàng quán shuǐ   矿泉水

KOOWNG KOOWN SHOOA

AT THE BAR

Bartender

Jiǔ bā zhāo dài   酒吧招待

J██-B██ J██ D██

The wine list, please.

Qíng gěi wǒ jiǔdān   请给我酒单

CH██NG G██ W██ J██-D██N

Cocktail

Jī wěi jiǔ   鸡尾酒

J██ W██ J██

On the rocks

Jiǎ bīng de   加冰的

J██ B██NG D██

Straight

Bù jiā bīng de   不加冰的

B██ J██ B██NG D██

With lemon

Jiā níng méng   加柠檬

J██ N██NG M██NG

PHRASEMAKER

I would like a glass of...

Qǐng gěi wǒ yī bēi... 请给我一杯

CH**EE**NG G**A** W**ah** **EE** B**A**...

▸ **champagne**

xiāng bīn 香槟

SH**EE**ah**NG B**EE**N

▸ **beer**

pí jiǔ 啤酒

P**EE** J**EE**O

▸ **wine**

pú táo jiǔ 葡萄酒

P**OO** T**OW** J**EE**O

▸ **red wine**

hóng pú táo jiǔ 红葡萄酒

H**O**NG P**OO** T**OW** J**EE**O

▸ **white wine**

bái pú táo jiǔ 白葡萄酒

B**I** P**OO** T**OW** J**EE**O

FAMILIAR FOODS

On the following pages you will
find lists of foods you are familiar
with, along with other information
such as basic utensils and preparation
instructions.

A polite way to get a waiter's or waitress's
attention is to say **Máfán ni?**, which means **May
I ask**, followed by your request and thank you.

May I ask?

Máfán ni?　麻烦你？

M⒜-F⒜N　N⒠

Please bring me...

Qǐng gěi wǒ...　请给我

CH⒠NG　G⒜　W⒜....

Thank you.

Xiè xie　谢谢你

SH⒠⒠　SH⒠⒠⒠　N⒠

STARTERS

Appetizers

Kāi wèi cài 开胃菜

K① W④ TS②

Bread and butter

Miàn bāo hé huáng yóu 面包和黄油

M(EE)(E)N B(OW) H(ih) H(OO)(ah)NG Y(O)

Cheese

Nǎi lào 奶酪

N① L(ow)

Fruit

Shuǐ guǒ 水果

SH(OO)(A) G(OO)(ah)

Salad

Sè lā 色拉

S(uh) L(ah)

Soup

Tāng 汤

T(ah)NG

MEAT

Bacon
Xūn ròu   熏肉

SH◉◉N R𝟢

Beef
Niú ròu   牛肉

N𝔼𝔼◉◉ R𝟢

Beef steak
Niú pái   牛排

N𝔼𝔼◉◉ P◉

Ham
Huǒ tuǐ   火腿

H◉◉◉ T◉◉◉

Lamb
Yáng ròu   羊肉

Y◉NG R𝟢

Pork
Zhū ròu   猪肉

J◉◉ R𝟢

Veal
Nèn niú ròu   嫩牛肉

N◉N N𝔼𝔼◉◉ R𝟢

POULTRY

Baked chicken

Kǎo jī   烤鸡

K⊚ⓦ Jⓔⓔ

Broiled chicken

Shāo jī   烧鸡

SHⓞⓦ Jⓔⓔ

Fried chicken

Zhá jī   炸鸡

Jⓐⓗ Jⓔⓔ

Duck

Yā zi (ròu)   鸭子（肉）

Yⓐⓗ DSⓔⓔ Rⓞ

Goose

É (ròu)   鹅（肉）

Ⓤ Rⓞ

Turkey

Huǒ jī (ròu)   火鸡（肉）

Hⓤⓤⓐⓗ Jⓔⓔ Rⓞ

SEAFOOD

Fish

Yú   鱼

Y_{oo}

Lobster

Lóng xiā   龙虾

L(O)NG   SH(EE)(ah)

Oysters

Háo   蚝 / mǔ lì   牡蛎

H(ow) / M(oo)-L(EE)

Salmon

Sān wén yú   三文鱼

S(ah)N   W(U)N   Y(oo)

Shrimp

Xiā   蚝

SH(EE)(ah)

Trout

Guì yú   鲑鱼

G(oo)(A)   Y(oo)

Tuna

Jīn qiāng yú   金枪鱼

J(EE)N   CH(EE)(ah)NG   Y(oo)

OTHER ENTREES

Sandwich

Sān míng zhì   三明治

S@N M@NG J@

Hot dog

Rè gǒu   热狗

B@ G@

Hamburger

Hàn bǎo bāo   汉堡包

H@N B@ B@

French fries

Zhá shǔ tiáo   炸薯条

J@ SH@ T@@

Pasta

Yì dà lì miàn tiáo   意大利面条

Y@ D@ L@ M@@N T@@

Pizza

Bǐ sà   比萨

B@ S@

VEGETABLES

Carrots

Hú luó bo   胡萝卜

H⊚⊚ L⊚⊚⊛ B⊙

Corn

Yù mǐ   玉米

Y⊚⊚ M⊛

Mushrooms

Mó gu   蘑菇

M⊙ G⊚⊚

Onions

Yáng cōng   洋葱

Y⊛NG TS⊙NG

Potato

Tǔ dòu   土豆

T⊚⊚ D⊘

Rice

(Da) Mǐ   （大）米

D⊛ M⊛

Tomato

Yī hóng chì   西红柿

SH⊛ H⊙NG SH⊘

FRUITS

Apple
Píng guǒ 苹果

PⒺNG GⓄⓄⓐ

Banana
Xiāng jiāo 香蕉

SHⒺⒺⓐNG JⒺⒺⓄⓌ

Grapes
Pú tao 葡萄

PⓄⓄ TⓄⓌ

Lemon
Níng méng 柠檬

NⒺNG MⓊNG

Orange
Jú zi 橘子 / Chéng zi 橙子

JⒺⓌ-DZⓊⒽ / CHⓊNG DZⓊⒽ

Strawberry
Cǎo méi 草莓

TSⓄⓌ MⒶ

Watermelon
Xī guā 西瓜

SHⒺⒺ GⓄⓄⓐ

DESSERT

Desserts

Tián diǎn   甜点

T︎EE︎N D︎EE︎N

Apple pie

Píng guǒ pài   苹果派

P︎ENG G︎OO︎ P︎

Cherry pie

Yīngtáo pài   樱桃派

Y︎ENG-T︎OW P︎

Pastries

Gāo diǎn   糕点

G︎OW D︎EE︎N

Candy

Táng   糖

T︎NG

Ice cream

Bīng jī líng   冰激凌

B**EE**NG J**EE** L**EE**NG

Ice cream cone

Bīng jī líng dàn juǎn   冰激凌蛋卷

B**EE**NG J**EE**

L**EE**NG D**ah**N J**oo**an**N

Chocolate

Qiǎo kē lì   巧克力

CH**EE**ow K**uh** L**EE**

Strawberry

Cǎo méi   草莓

TS**ow** M**A**

Vanilla

Xiāng cǎo   香草

SH**EE**uhNG TS**ow**

CONDIMENTS

Butter
Huáng yóu   黄油

H⬤⬤NG Y⬤

Ketchup
Fān qié jiàng   番茄酱

F⬤N CH⬤⬤ J⬤⬤NG

Mayonnaise
Dàn húang jìang   蛋黄酱

D⬤N H⬤⬤NG J⬤⬤NG

Mustard
Jìe mò   芥末

J⬤⬤ M⬤

Salt	Pepper
Yán 盐	Hú jiāo 胡椒
Y⬤N	H⬤ J⬤⬤

Sugar
Táng   糖

T⬤NG

Vinegar	Oil
Cù 醋	Yóu 油
TS⬤	Y⬤

SETTINGS

A cup

Yí gè chá bēi 一个茶杯

Ⓔ Ⓖuh CHⓐh BⒶ

A glass

Yí gè bōli bēi 一个玻璃杯

Ⓔ Ⓖuh BⓄ-LⒺ BⒶ

A spoon

Yì bǎ sháo zi 一把勺子

Ⓔ Bⓐh SHⓞw DSⓊr

A fork

Yì bǎ chā zi 一把叉子

Ⓔ Bⓐh CHⓐh DSⓊr

A knife

Yì bǎ cān dāo 一把餐刀

Ⓔ Bⓐh TSⓐhN Dⓞw

A plate

Yí gè pán zi 一个盘子

Ⓔ Ⓖuh PⓐhN DSⓊr

A napkin

Yī zhāng cān jīn zhǐ 一张餐巾纸

Ⓔ JⓐhNG TSⓐhN JⒺN JⓊr

HOW DO YOU WANT IT COOKED?

Baked

Kǎo de   烤的

K⊚w D⓪h

Broiled

Zhǔ de   煮的

J⊚⊚ D⓪h

Steamed

Zhēng de   蒸的

J⓪NG D⓪h

Fried

Zhá de   炸的

J⓪ D⓪h

Rare

Shēng yī diǎn de   生一点的

SH⓪NG ⓔⓔ DⓔⓔⓢN D⓪h

Medium

Zhōng děng de   中等的

J⊙NG D⊙NG D⓪h

Well done

Shú de   熟的

SH⊚⊚ D⓪h

PROBLEMS

I didn't order this.

Wǎ méi yǒu yào zhè ge.   我没有要这个。

W@h M@ Y① Y@w J@h G@h

Is the bill correct?

Zhè zhàng dān duì ma?   这账单对吗？

J@h ZH@NG D@hN D@@④ M@h

Bring me...

Qǐng gěi wǒ...   请给我

CH@NG G@ W①...

PRAISE

Thank you for the delicious meal.

Hěn hǎo chī   很好吃

H@N H@w CH@

GETTING AROUND

Getting around in a foreign country can be an adventure in itself! Taxi and bus drivers do not always speak English, so it is essential to be able to give simple directions. The words and phrases in this chapter will help you get where you're going.

- China is considered a safe place to visit and major cities have good transportation including public buses, tour buses, mini buses, and taxis.

- Taxis are always metered. Taxis are fairly cheap and reliable and are the best way to get around.

- Have a map or the address you want to go to written down in Chinese.

- Remember to take a business card from your hotel to give to the taxi driver on your return.

- Train tickets can be booked at your hotel or at the Foreigners' Ticket Office in the Beijing Railway Station and the West Station.

KEY WORDS

Airport

Fēi jī chǎng   飞机场

FⒶ Jⓗ CHⓎNG

Bus Station / Bus Stop

Qì chē zhàn   汽车站

CH⒴ CHⓤ JⓑN

Car Rental Agency

Zū chē chù   租车处

JⓏ CHⓤ CHⓏ

Subway Station

Dì tiě zhàn   地铁站

DⒶ TⒶⒶⒶ JⓑN

Taxi Stand

Chū zū chē zhàn   出租车站

CHⓏⓗ DSⓏ CHⓤ JⓑN

Train Station

Huǒ chē zhàn   火车站

HⓏⓏⓑ CHⓤ JⓑN

AIR TRAVEL

Airport

Fēi jī chǎng　　飞机场

F(A)　J(Ur)　CH(ah)NG

A one-way ticket, please.

Qǐng gěi wǒ yī zhāng dān chéng chē piào.

请给我一张单程车票

CH(EE)NG　G(A)　W(ah)

(EE)　J(ah)NG　D(ah)N

CH(uh)NG　CH(uh)　P(EE)(ow)

A round trip ticket.

Shuāng chéng　/　Wǎng fǎn chē piào.

双程（往返）车票

SH(oo)(ah)NG　CH(uh)NG

W(ah)NG　F(ah)N　CH(uh)　P(EE)(ow)

First class

Tóu děng cāng　　头等舱

T(O)　D(uh)NG　TS(ah)N

How much do I owe?

Wǒ yào fù duō shǎo qián?　　我要付多少钱？

W(ah)　Y(ow)　F(oo)　D(oo)(ah)　SH(ow)　CH(EE)(n)N

PHRASEMAKER

I would like a seat...

Wǒ xiǎng yào gè...　我想要个

W@h SH(EE)@hNG Y@w G@h...

▸ **in first class**

tóu děng cāng de zuò wèi　头等舱的座位

T© D@hNG TS@hNG D@h
DS@@@h W@

▸ **next to the window**

kào chuāng hù de zuò wèi　靠窗户的座位

K@w CH@@@hNG H@ D@h
DS@@@h W@

▸ **on the aisle**

kào gùodào de zuò wèi　靠过道的座位

K@w G@@@h-D@w D@h
DS@@@h W@

▸ **near the exit**

kào jìn chū kǒu de zuò wèi　靠近出口的 座位

K@w J@N CH@@ K© D@h
DS@@@h W@

BY BUS

Bus

Gōng gòng qì chē   公共汽车

G⊙NG G⊙NG CH㋐ CH⒰

Where is the bus stop?

Gōng gòng qì chē zhàn zài nǎ lǐ?
公共汽车站在哪里？

G⊙NG G⊙NG CH㋐ CH⒰
J㋐N DS⊘ N㋐-L㋐

Do you go to…?

Nǐ qù...?   你去

N㋐ CH⊚

What is the fare?

Pìaojìa dūo shǎo?   票价多少？

P㋐⊚-J㋐㋐ D⊚ah SH⊚

Do I need exact change?

Xū yào zhèng hǎo de líng qián ma?
需要正好的零钱吗？

SH⊚ Y⊚ J⊚NG
H⊚ D⒰ L㋐NG
CH㋐㋐N M㋐

PHRASEMAKER

Which bus goes to…

Nǎ liàng qì chē… 哪辆汽车去

N⒜ L⒠⒪NG CH⒠ CH⒰

▶ **Tian'anmen square?**

Tiān'ānmēn guǎng chǎng? 天安门广场

T⒠⒜N ⒜N M⒰N
G⒪⒜NG CH⒜NG

▶ **the beach?**

hǎi tān? 海滩

H⒤ T⒜N

▶ **the Forbidden City?**

giù gòng? 故宫?

G⒪ G⒪NG

BY CAR

Can you help me?

Nǐ néng bāng wǒ ma?   你能帮我吗

N⒠ N⒪NG
B⒜NG W⒜ M⒜

My car won't start.

Wǒ de chē bù néng kāi le.   我的车不能开了?

W⒜ D⒰ CH⒰
B⒪⒪ N⒪NG
K⒤ L⒰

Can you fix it?

Nǐ néng xiū hǎo tā ma?   你能修好它吗?

N⒠ N⒪NG
SH⒠⒪ H⒪W T⒜ M⒜

What will it cost?

Yào duō shǎo qián?   要多少钱?

Y⒪W D⒪⒪⒜ SH⒪W J⒠⒠N

How long will it take?

Yào duō cháng shí jiān?   要多长时间

Y⒪W D⒪⒪⒜ CH⒪NG SH⒤ J⒠⒠N
SH⒤ J⒠⒠N

PHRASEMAKER

Please check…

Qǐng jiǎn chá... 请检查

CH**E**NG J**EE**N CH**ah**...

▸ **the battery**

diàn chí 电池

D**EE**N CH**ur**

▸ **the brakes**

shā chē 车

SH**ah** CH**uh**

▸ **the oil**

jī yóu 机油

J**EE** Y**O**

▸ **the tires**

lún tāi 轮胎

L**oo**N T**I**

▸ **the water**

shuǐ xiāng 水箱

SH**oo**A SH**EE**ahNG

SUBWAYS AND TRAINS

Where is the train station?

Huǒ chē zhàn zài nǎ lǐ?   火车站在哪里？

H⓪⓪ⓐⓗ CHⓤⓘ J🅐N DS🅘 N🅐ⓗ L🅔🅔

A one-way ticket, please.

Qǐng gěi wǒ yī zhāng dān chéng chē piào.

请给我一张单程车票

CH🅔NG G🅐 W🅐ⓗ
🅔🅔 J🅐ⓗNG D🅐ⓗN
CH🅦NG CHⓤⓗ P🅔🅔⓪ⓦ

A round trip ticket.

Shuāng chéng / Wǎng fǎn chē piào.

双程（往返）车票

SH⓪⓪🅐ⓗNG CH🅦NG
W🅐NG F🅐ⓗN CHⓤⓗ P🅔🅔⓪ⓦ

First class

Tóu děng cāng   头等舱

T🅞 DⓤⓗNG TS🅐ⓗN

Second class

Èr děng cāng   二等舱

🅐ⓗR̲ DⓤⓗNG TS🅐ⓗNG

Try to ask for first class.

What is the fare?

Piào jià dūo shǎo?　票价多少？

P(EE)(OW) J(EE)(ah) D(OO)(ah) SH(OW)

Is this seat taken?

Zhè gè zuò wèi yǒu rén ma?　这个座位有人吗？

J(uh) G(uh) DS(OO)(ay) W(ay)
Y(O) R(ön)N M(ah)

Do I have to change trains?

Wǒ bì xū huàn huǒ chē ma?　我必须换火车吗？

W(ah) B(EE) SH(OO) H(OO)(ah)N
H(OO)(ah) CH(uh) M(ah)

Where are we?

Wǒmén (xiàn zài) zài nǎ?　我们（现在）在哪？

W(ah)-M(ön)N (SH(EE)(ah)N DS(i))
DS(i) N(ah)

BY TAXI

Please call a taxi for me.

Qǐng bāng wǒ jiào liàng chē   请帮我叫辆车

CH**ⒺⒺ**NG B**ⓐⓗ**NG W**ⓐⓗ** J**ⒺⒺⓄⓌ**
L**ⒺⒺⓐⓗ**NG CH**ⓤⓗ**

Are you available?

Nǐ yǒu kòng mā?   你有空吗？

N**ⒺⒺ** Y**Ⓞ** K**Ⓞ**NG M**ⓐⓗ**

I want to go…

Wǒ xiǎng qù...   我想去

W**ⓐⓥ** SH**ⒺⒺⓐⓗ**NG CH**ⓄⓄ**...

Stop here, please.

Qǐng zài zhè'er tíng yì xià.   请在这儿停一下

CH**ⒺⒺ**NG DS**Ⓘ** J**ⓤⓗ**R̲
T**ⒺⒺ**NG **ⒺⒺ** SH**ⒺⒺⓐⓗ**

Please wait.

Qǐng děng yì huǐ 'er.   请等一会儿

CH**ⒺⒺ**NG D**ⓤⓗ**NG **ⒺⒺ** H**ⓄⓄ**-**ⓐⓗ**R̲

How much do I owe?

Wǒ yào fù duō shǎo qián?   我要付多少钱？

W**ⓐⓗ** Y**ⓄⓌ** F**Ⓞ** D**ⓄⓄⓐⓗ** SH**ⓄⓌ** CH**ⒺⒺⓄ**N

PHRASEMAKER

The simplest way to get to where you want to go is to name the destination and simply say **please**.

▸ **This address...**

Dì zhǐ ...   地址

D㊎ J㊣...

Have someone at your hotel write down the address for you in Chinese characters.

▸ **This hotel...**

Jǔ diàn...   酒店

J㋎ D㊎㋆N...

▸ **Airport...**

Fēi jī chǎng...   飞机场

F㋐ J㊎ CH㋐NG...

▸ **Subway station...**

Dì tiè zhàn...   地铁站

D㊎ T㊎㋆ J㋐N...

...please.

...qǐng.   请

...CH㋐NG

SHOPPING

Whether you plan a major shopping spree or just need to purchase some basic necessities, the following information is useful.

- You can find duty-free shops in airports, major trains stations, and tourist cities.

- Prices are usually cheaper in duty-free shops and you can find money exchange shops here.

- There are also state-run "friendship" stores that carry quality merchandise but less selection.

- Beijing offers a variety of arts and crafts, outdoor markets, and large department stores and bargaining in markets is welcomed.

- Always remember to ask for receipts. You will need to show your passport to the sales assistant when you purchase the goods to allow him or her to fill out the VAT form.

- It's best not to pack your purchases into your check-in luggage.

- At the airport, get your VAT form stamped at the VAT refund desk.

KEY WORDS

Credit card

Xìn yòng kǎ 信用卡

SHEEN YONG Kah

Money

Qián 钱

CHEEON

Receipt

Shōu jù 收据

SHO JOO

Sale

Dǎ zhé 打折

Dah JUH

Store

Shāng dìan 商店

SHAhNG DEEON

Traveler's checks

Lǚxíng zhīpìao 旅行支票

Lew SHEENG JEE PEEOW

USEFUL PHRASES

Do you sell…?

Nǐ mài...?   你卖

N㋐ M㋐…

Do you have…?

Nǐ yǒu...?   你有

N㋐ Y㋐…

I want to buy.

Wǒ xiǎng mǎi.   我想买

W㋐ SH㋐㋐NG M㋐

How much?

Duō shǎo qián?   多少钱？

D㋐㋐ SH㋐ CH㋐㋐N

When are the shops open?

Shāng diàn shénme shíhuà kāi mén?
商店什么时候开门？

SH㋐NG D㋐㋐N
SH㋐N-M㋐ SH㋐-H㋐㋐
K㋐ M㋐N

No, thank you.

Bù, xiè xie.   不 谢谢

B⊚⊙ SH⒠⒠⒠ SH⒠⒠⒠

I'm just looking.

Wǒ zhǐ shì kàn kàn.   我只是看看

W⓪ Jⓤr SH⓪ K⓪N K⓪N

Is it very expensive?

Zhè hěn guì ma?   这很贵吗？

J⓪ H⓾N G⓸⓸ⓐ Mⓐ

Can't you give me a discount?

Nǐ kě yǐ gěi wǒ dǎ zhé ma?   你可以给我打折吗？

N⒠⒠ K⓸⓸ ⒠⒠

Gⓐ Wⓐ Dⓐ

J⓾ Mⓐ

I'll take it.

Wǒ yào le!   我要了！

Wⓐ Y⓸ L⓾

I'd like a receipt, please.

Qǐng gěi wǒ shou jù.   请给我收据

CI⓸NG Gⓐ Wⓐ

SH⓪ J⓸

SHOPS AND SERVICES

Bakery

Gāobǐng dìan　糕饼店

G⒪W B⒠NG D⒠⒠⒪N

Bank

Yín háng　银行

Y⒠N H⒜NG

Hair salon

Fà láng　发廊

F⒜ L⒜NG

Barbershop

Lǐfà dìan　理发店

L⒠⒠-F⒜ D⒠⒠⒪N

Jewelry store

Shǒu shì dìan　理发店

SH⒪ SH⒰ D⒠⒠⒪N

Bookstore

Shū dìan　书店

SH⒪⒪ D⒠⒠⒪N

News stand

Bào tíng　报亭

B⒪W T⒠NG

Camera shop

Zhào xìang qì cái shāngdìan　照相器材商店

J⒪W SH⒠⒠⒜NG

CH⒠⒠ TS⒤

SH⒜NG D⒠⒠⒪N

Pharmacy

Yào dìan　约店

Y⒪W D⒠⒠⒪N

SHOPPING LIST

On the following pages you will find some common items you may need to purchase on your trip.

Aspirin
A sī pī lín　阿斯匹林

ⓐⓗ Sⓔⓔ Pⓔⓔ LⓔⓔN

Cigarettes
Xiáng yān　香烟

SHⓔⓔⓐⓗNG YⓐⓗN

Deodorant
Chú chòujì　除臭剂

CHⓞⓞ CHⓞ-Jⓤⓡ

Dress
Yī fú　衣服

ⓔⓔ Fⓞⓞ

Film
Jiāo juǎn　胶卷

Jⓔⓔⓞⓦ JⓞⓞⓐⓝN

Perfume

Xiāng shuǐ   香水

SH(EE)(ah)NG SH(oo)(A)

Razor blades

Tì dāo   剃刀

T(EE) D(ow)

Shampoo

Xiāng bō   香波

SH(EE)(ah)NG B(O)

Shaving cream

Tì xū gāo   剃须刀

T(EE) SH(oo) G(ow)

Shirt

Chèn yī   衬衣

CH(u)N (EE)

Sunglasses

tài yáng jìng / mò jìng   太阳镜 / 墨镜

T**Ⓘ** Y**ⓐ**NG J**ⓔ**NG / M**Ⓞ** J**ⓔ**NG

Suntan oil

fáng shài shuāng   防晒霜

F**ⓐ**NG SH**Ⓘ** SH**ⓞⓞⓐ**NG

Toothbrushes

yá shuā   牙刷

Y**ⓐ** SH**ⓞⓞⓐ**

Toothpaste

yá gāo   牙膏

Y**ⓐ** G**ⓞⓦ**

Water (bottled)

chún jìng shuǐ   纯净水

CH**ⓞ**N J**ⓔ**NG SH**ⓞⓞⒶ**

Water (mineral)

kuàng quán shuǐ   矿泉水

K**ⓞⓞⓐ**NG CH**ⓞⓞⓐ**N SH**ⓞⓞⒶ**

ESSENTIAL SERVICES

THE BANK

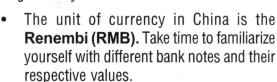

As a traveler in a foreign country your primary contact with banks will be to exchange money.

- The unit of currency in China is the **Renembi (RMB).** Take time to familiarize yourself with different bank notes and their respective values.

- It is a good idea to carry traveler's checks rather than cash. Don't display money in public.

- Have your passport handy when changing money. Cash or traveler's checks can be exchanged for Chinese currency at banks and licensed exchange facilities of the Bank of China.

- Money exchanges are also available at major airports and hotels.

- ATMs are readily available in major cities.

- Most major credit cards are accepted; however, it is a good idea to check with your bank to see if your credit card is accepted.

KEY WORDS

Bank

Yín háng   银行

YⒺN HⓐNG

Exchange office

Huàn waìbì   换外币

HⓄⓄNⓐ/N WⓄ-BⒺⒺ

Money

Qián   钱

CHⒺⒺⓇN

Money order

Huì piào   汇票

HⓄⓄⒶ PⒺⒺⓆw

Traveler's check

Lǔ xíng zhī piào   旅行支票

LⒺw SHⒺNG JⓊr PⒺⒺⓆw

USEFUL PHRASES

Where is the bank?

Yín háng zài nǎ?   银行在哪？

YⒺN HⓐNG DSⓄ Nⓐⓗ

What time does the bank open?

Yín háng jǐ diǎn kāi mén?   银行几点开门？

YⒺN HⓐNG JⒺ
DⒺⒺⓔN K①-MⓤⓝN

Where is the exchange office?

Zài nǎ huàn waìbì?   在哪换外币？

DSⓄ Nⓐⓗ HⓄⓄⓐN WⓄ-BⒺ

What time does the exchange office open?

Huàn waìbì de dìfāng jǐ diǎn kāi mén?
换外币的地方几点开门？

HⓄⓄⓐN WⓄ-BⒺ Dⓤⓗ DⒺ-FⓐⓗNG
JⒺ DⒺⒺⓔN K①-MⓤⓝN

Can I change dollars here?

Wǒ kě yǐ zài zhè huàn měi yuán ma?
我可以在这换美元吗？

Wⓐⓗ Kⓞⓤ ⒺⒺ DSⓄ
HⓄⓄⓐN MⒶ YⓄⓄⓐN Mⓐⓗ

What is the exchange rate?

Huì lǜ shì duō shǎo?　汇率是多少?

H⓪⓪Ⓐ　LⒺⓌ　SHⓊ　D⓪⓪ⓐh　SHⓄⓌ

I would like large bills.

Wǒ　xiǎng yào da miàn e chāo piào.
我想要大面额钞票

WⓐⒽ　SHⒺⒺⓐhNG　YⓄⓌ
Dⓐh　MⒺⒺⒶN　Ⓔ̃　CHⓄⓌ　PⒺⒺⓄⓌ

I would like small bills.

Wǒ xiǎng yào xiǎo miàn e chāo piào.
我想要小面额钞票

WⓐⒽ　SHⒺⒺⓐhNG　YⓄⓌ
SHⒺⒺⓄⓌ　MⒺⒺⒶN
Ⓔ̃　CHⓄⓌ　PⒺⒺⓄⓌ

I need change.

Wǒ xū yào líng qián.　我需要零钱

WⓐⒽ　SHⓄⓄ　YⓄⓌ
LⒺNG　CHⒺⒺⒺ̃N

Do you have an ATM?

Zhè lǐ yǒu tí kuǎn jī ma?　这里有提款机吗?

JⓊⒽ　LⒺⒺ　YⓄ　TⒺⒺ
K⓪⓪ⓐhN　JⒺⒺ　MⓐⒽ

POST OFFICE

If you are planning on sending letters and postcards, be sure to send them early so that you don't arrive home before they do.

KEY WORDS

Air mail

Háng kóng yóu jiàn   航空邮件

H⊛NG K⊙NG Y⊙ J⒠⒡N

Letter

Xìn   信

SH⒠N

Post office

Yóu jú   邮局

Y⊙ J⒨

Postcard

Míng xìn piàn   明信片

M⒠NG SH⒠N P⒠⒡N

Stamp

Yóu piào   邮票

Y⊙ P⒠⒵

USEFUL PHRASES

Where is the post office?

Yóu jú zài nǎ?   邮局在哪？

YO J⓪ DS⓪ N⓪

What time does the post office open?

Yòu jú jǐ diǎn kāi mén?   邮局几点开门？

YO J⓪ Jⓔⓔ

DⓔⓔⓔN K①-M⓪N

I need…

Wǒ xū yào...   我需要

W① SH⓪ Y⓪

I need stamps.

Wǒ xū yào yóu piào.   我需要 邮票

W① SH⓪ Y⓪ YO Pⓔⓔ⓪

I need an envelope.

Wǒ xū yào xìn fēng.   我需要 信封

W① SH⓪ Y⓪ SHⓔN F⓪NG

I need a pen.

Wǒ xū yào bǐ.   我需要 笔

W① SH⓪ Y⓪ Bⓔⓔ

TELEPHONE

Placing phone calls in China can be
a test of will and stamina! Besides
the obvious language barriers, service
can vary greatly from one town to the
next.

- Direct long-distance dials (DDD) and
  international calls (IDD) can be made
  from hotel rooms or roadside telephone
  kiosks.

- International calls can also be made from
  main communications offices.

- Public phones are available in many shops,
  restaurants, and on the street.

- In some large cities, you can buy IP phone
  cards which can save you money.

- Internet services are found in cyber cafes
  and in major hotels.

KEY WORDS

Information

Chá hào tái 查号台

CHah How Ti

Long distance

Cháng tú 长途

CHahNG Too

Operator

Jiē xiàn yuán 接线员

JEEe SHEEaN YOOaN

Phone book

Diàn huà běn 电话本

DEEaN HOOah BuN

Public telephone

Góng yòng diàn huà 公用电话

GONG YONG DEEaN HOOah

USEFUL PHRASES

Where is the telephone?

Diàn huà zài nǎ lǐ?   电话在哪里

D◉◉◉N H◍◍◍ DS◍ N◍-L◉◉

Where is the public telephone?

Gōng yōng diàn huà zài ná lǐ?   公用电话在哪里?

G◍NG Y◍NG D◉◉◉N H◍◍◍
DS◍ N◍ L◉◉

May I use your telephone?

Wǒ kě yǐ yòng yí xià nǐ de diàn huà ma?   .
我可以用一下你的电话吗?

W◍ K◍ ◉◉
Y◍NG ◉ SH◉◉◍
N◉◉ D◍
D◉◉◉N H◍◍◍ M◍

Operator, I don't speak Chinese.

Jiē xiàn yuán, wǒ bú huì jiǎng hànyǔ.

接线员,我不会讲汉语

J◉◉◉ SH◉◉◉N Y◍◍◍N
W◍ B◍ H◍◍
J◉◉◉NG H◍N-Y◍

I want to call this number...

Wǒ xiǎng dǎ zhè gè hào...   我想打这个号

Wⓐ SHⓔⓔⓐNG Dⓐh
Jⓤ Gⓤ Hⓞⱳ...

1	2	3
yī 一 ⓔⓔ	èr 二 ⓐⓡ	sān 三 SⓐhN
4	5	6
sì 四 Sⓤⱳ	wǔ 五 Wⓤⓤ	liù 六 Lⓔⓔⓞ
7	8	9
qī 七 CHⓔⓔ	bā 八 Bⓐh	jiǔ 九 Jⓔⓔⓞ
✱	0 líng LⓔNG	#

SIGHTSEEING AND ENTERTAINMENT

Beijing is the capital and the most modern of cities in the Republic of China. It is home to several ancient palaces, temples, and historical and cultural sites.

CITIES IN CHINA

Beijing 北京
Popular sites in China include the Great Wall, Tian'anmen Square, one of the largest squares in the world built in 1417, and The Forbidden City now known as The Palace Museum.

Shanghai 上海
Shanghai boasts western influence with twenty-story-high buildings reaching skyward and showered with many hotel complexes and villas.

Hong Kong 香港
Hong Kong's natural beauty, rich culture, and accessibility make this city a great gateway to your China travels. Enjoy a beautiful view of the city while riding the Star Ferry through Victoria Harbor.

Xi'an 西安
The city where Chinese culture began its roots and where you can visit the fantastic Qin Terracotta Warrior Museum.

KEY WORDS

Admission

Rùchǎng 入场

R<u>OO</u> CH<u>a</u>NG

Map

Dì tú 地图

D<u>EE</u> T<u>OO</u>

Reservation

Yù dìng 预定

Y<u>OO</u> D<u>EE</u>NG

Ticket

Piào 票

P<u>EE</u><u>OW</u>

Tour

Lǚ xíng 旅行 (or) Lǚ yóu 旅游

L<u>ew</u> SH<u>EE</u>NG / L<u>ew</u> Y<u>O</u>

Tour guide

Lǚ yóu zhǐ nán 旅游指南

L<u>ew</u> Y<u>O</u> J<u>Ur</u> N<u>a</u>N

USEFUL PHRASES

Where is the tourist agency?

Lǔ xíng shè zài nǎ?   旅行社在哪？

L⒠ⓦ SH⒠ⓝG SH⒲ DS⒵ N⒜ⓗ

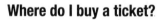

Where do I buy a ticket?

Wǒ zài nǎ mǎi mén piào?   我在哪买门票？

W⒜ⓗ DS⒵ N⒜ⓝ M⒤ M⒲N P⒠ⓔⓦ

How much?

Duō shǎo qián?   多少钱？

D⒪⒪⒜ⓗ SH⒪ⓦ CH⒠ⓔⓢN

How long?

Duō cháng?   多长时间

D⒪⒪⒜ⓗ CH⒜ⓝG

When?

Shénme shíhòu?   什么时候？

SH⒠ⓝ-M⒰ⓗ SH⒲-H⒵

Where?

Náli?   哪里？

N⒜ⓗ-L⒠ⓔ

Do I need reservations?

Wǒ xū yào yù yuē ma?   我需要预约吗？

Wah SHoo Yow
Yoo Yooĕ Mah

Does the guide speak English?

Zhè gè dǎo yóu jiǎng yīng yǔ ma?
这个导游讲英语吗？

Jŭ Gŭ Dow
Yo JeeĕNG
YeeNG Yoo Mah

How much do children pay?

Xiǎo hái fù duō shǎo qián?   小孩付多少钱？

SHeeow Hĭ Foo
Dooah SHow CHeeĕN

I need your help.

Wǒ xū yào nǐ bāng máng.   我需要 你的帮忙

Wah SHoo Yow Nee Bahng Mahng

Thank you.

Xièxie nì.   谢谢你

SHeeĕ SHeeă Nee

PHRASEMAKER

I'm looking for...

Wǒ zài nǎ néng zhǎo dào...   我在哪能找到

W@h DS@ N@h
N@NG J@w D@w...

▸ **the Summer Palace**

yí hé yuán   颐和园

@ H@ Y@@N

The Summer Palace is a popular local spot featuring mythical paintings, gardens and Kunming Lake.

▸ **a Tea House**

lǎo shě chá guǎn   老舍茶馆

L@w SH@h CH@ G@@N

Tea houses offer famous Beijing Opera performances and Chinese acrobats — a wonderful entertainment experience. They serve tea, snacks, and food.

▸ **the Great Wall**

chíng chéng   长城

CH@NG CH@NG

▶ **a swimming pool**

yóu yǒng chí   游泳池

YO̱   YO̱NG   CHO̱

▶ **a movie theater**

diàn yǐng yuàn   看电影吗

DEE̱N   YEE̱NG   YOO̱N

▶ **a health club**

jiàn shēn jù lè bù   健身俱乐部

JEE̱N   SHU̱N   JOO   LU̱   BOO

▶ **a tennis court**

wǎng qiú chǎng   网球场

WA̱NG   CHEE̱OO   CHA̱NG

▶ **a golf course**

gāo ěr fū qiú chǎng   高尔夫球场

GOW   A̱R   FOO   CHEE̱OO   CHA̱NG

HEALTH

Hopefully you will not need medical attention on your trip. If you do, it is important to communicate basic information regarding your condition.

- Check with your insurance company before leaving home to find out if you are covered in a foreign country. You may want to purchase traveler's insurance before leaving home.

- If you take prescription medicine, carry your prescription with you. Have your prescriptions translated into simplified Chinese writing before you leave home.

- Take a small first-aid kit with you. You may want to include basic cold and anti-diarrhea medications. However, you should be able to find most items like aspirin locally.

- In most cases foreigners in large cities like Beijing are sent to the best hospitals and treated by the best doctors in China.

- Hospitals are open seven days a week and sometimes require fees be paid in advance.

KEY WORDS

Ambulance

Jiù hù chē   救护车

J(EE)(oo) H(oo) CH(uh)

Dentist

Yá yī   牙医

Y(ah) (EE)

Doctor

Yī shēng   医生

(EE) SH(uh)NG

Emergency

Jí zhěn   急诊

J(EE) J(uh)N

Hospital

Yī yuàn   医院

(EE) Y(oo)(ah)N

Prescription

Chù fāng   处方

CH(oo) F(ah)NG

USEFUL PHRASES

I am sick.

Wǒ bìng le.   我病了

W(ah) B(ee)NG L(uh)

I need a doctor.

Wǒ yào kàn yī shēng.   我要看医生

W(ah) Y(ow) K(ah)N (ee) SH(uh)NG

It's an emergency!

Zhè shì jí zhěn!   这是急诊！

J(uh) SH(u) J(ee) J(uh)N

Where is the nearest hospital?

Zuì jìn dè yī yuàn zài nǎ lǐ?   最近的医院在哪里？

DS(oo)(a) J(ee)N D(uh)
(ee) Y(oo)(ah)N DS(i) N(ah) L(ee)

Call an ambulance!

Qǐng jiào jiù hù chē!   请叫救护车！

CH(ee)NG J(ee)(ow) H(oo) CH(uh)

I'm allergic to…

Wǒ duì…guò mǐn.   我对。。。过敏

Wah Doo(A)…Goo(ah) M(EE)N

I'm pregnant.

Wǒ huái yùn le.   我怀孕了

Wah Hoo(y) Y(oo)N L(uh)

I'm diabetic.

Wǒ yǒu táng niào bìng.   我有糖尿病

Wah Yo T(ah)NG
N(EE)(ow) B(ee)NG

I have a heart condition.

Wǒ xīnzàng bù hǎo.   我心脏不好

Wah SH(EE)N-DS(ah)NG Boo How

I have high blood pressure.

Wǒ yǒu gāo xuě yā.   我有高血压

Wah Yo
G(ow) SH(oo)(e) Y(ah)

I have low blood pressure.

Wǒ yǒu dī xuě ya.   我有低血压

Wah Yo
D(EE) SH(oo)(e) Y(ah)

PHRASEMAKER

I need...

Wǒ yào...   我要

W Y...

▶ **a doctor**

kàn yī shēng   看医生

KN      SHNG

▶ **a dentist**

kàn yá yī   看牙医

KN   Y

▶ **a nurse**

yí gè hù shì   一个护士

   G   H   SH

▶ **an optician**

yàn guāng shī   验光师

YN   GNG   SH

▶ **a pharmacist**

yàojì shī   药剂师

Y-J   SH

PHRASEMAKER
(AT THE PHARMACY)

Do you have...

Nǐ yǒu...   你有

NⒺ YⓄ...

▶ **aspirin?**

ā sī pī lín ma?   阿斯匹林吗？

ⓐⓗ SⒺ PⒺ LⒺN Mⓐⓗ

▶ **Band-Aids?**

chuàng kě tiē ma?   创可贴 吗？

CHⓄⓄⓐ⁄ⓝNG KⓄⓤ TⒺⒺⓔ Mⓐⓗ

▶ **cough syrup?**

zhǐké táng jiāng ma?   止咳糖浆 吗？

JⓊⓡ-KⓊⓝ TⓐⓝNG JⒺⒺⓐⓗNG Mⓐⓗ

▶ **ear drops?**

dī ěr yè ma?   滴耳液 吗？

DⒺ ⓐⓗⒷ YⓄⓤ Mⓐⓗ

▶ **eye drops?**

yǎn yào shuǐ ma?   眼药水 吗？

YⓐⓗN YⓄⓦ SHⓄⓄⒶ Mⓐⓗ

BUSINESS TRAVEL

It is important to show appreciation and interest in another person's language and culture, particularly when doing business. A few well-pronounced phrases can make a great impression.

- Exchanging business cards is very important, so be sure to bring a good supply with you.

- It is a good idea to have your business card printed in simplified Chinese and engraved in gold (which implies status).

- Present your business card with the Chinese side facing up, holding it in both hands followed by a handshake. It is a good idea to wait for the recipient to offer the handshake first. He or she may defer to a nod.

- When you receive a card, be sure to examine it and then place it in your card case.

- Business dress is conservative for both men and women and bright-colored clothing is considered inappropriate.

- Gift giving is not a part of Chinese business culture and in most cases will be declined.

- It is not a good idea to wave about or use your hands while speaking.

KEY WORDS

Appointment

Yù yuē 预约

Y Y

Business card

Míng piàn 名片

MNG PN

Meeting

Huì yì 会议

H

Marketing

Shì chǎng 市场

SH CHNG

Office

Bàn gòng shì 办公室

BN GNG SH

Presentation

Huì bào 汇报

H B

Telephone

Diàn huà 电话

DN H

USEFUL PHRASES

I have an appointment.

Wǒ yoǔ yù yuē.   我有约会

W⒜h   Y◯   Y⒪⒪   Y⒪⒪⒠

My name is…(your name). Pleased to meet you.

Wǒ jiào... hěn gào xìng jiàn dào nǐ.
我叫... 很高兴见到你

W⒜h   J⒠⒠⒪w ....(your name)

H⒰h N   G⒪w   SH⒠⒠NG   J⒠⒠⒠N   D⒪w   N⒠⒠

Here is my card.

Zhè shì wǒ de míng piàn.   这是我的名片

J⒰h   SH⒰h

W⒜h   D⒰h   M⒠⒠NG   P⒠⒠⒠N

Exchanging business cards should be done with care, holding
your card with both hands with Chinese printing facing the
recipient. It is normal to follow with a handshake.

Can we get an interpreter?

Kě yǐ zhǎo dào yí gē fān yì ma?
可以找到一个翻译吗？

K⒪w   ⒠⒠   J⒪w   D⒪w   ⒠⒠   G⒪w

F⒜h N   ⒠⒠   M⒜h

Can you write your address for me?

Nǐ kě yǐ xiě xià nǐ de dì zhǐ ma?

你可以写下你的地址吗？

NⒺ KⓄⓊ Ⓔ

SHⒺⓔ SHⒺⒶⓗ NⒺ Dⓤⓗ

DⒺ JⓊⓇ MⒶⓗ

Can you write your phone number?

Nǐ kě yǐ xiě xià nǐ de diàn huà ma?

你可以写下你的电话吗？

NⒺ KⓄⓊ Ⓔ

SHⒺⓔ SHⒺⒶⓗ NⒺ Dⓤⓗ

DⒺⒺN HⓄⓄⒶⓗ MⒶⓗ

This is my phone number.

Zhè shì wǒ de diàn huà.   这是我的电话

JⓊⓗ SHⓊ WⒶⓗ Dⓤⓗ

DⒺⒺN HⓄⓄⒶ

His/Her name is...

Ta jiào...   她叫

TⒶⓗ JⒺⓄⓌ...

Good-bye.

Zaì jiàn.   再见

DSⒶ JⒺⒶN

PHRASEMAKER

I need.

Wǒ xū yào...   我需要

W@h SH@ Y@w...

▶ **a computer**

diàn nǎo   电脑

D@@@N N@w

▶ **a copy machine**

fù yìn jī   复印机

F@ Y@@N J@

▶ **a conference room**

hiu yì shǐ   复印室

H@@@ @ SH@

▶ **a fax or fax machine**

chuán zhēn jí   传真机

CH@@@N J@N J@

▶ **an interpreter**

fān yì   翻译

F@hN @

▸ **a lawyer**

lǜ shī 律师

L SH

▸ **a notary**

gōng zhèng yuán 公证员

GNG JNG YN

▸ **a pen**

bǐ 笔

B

▸ **stamps**

yóu piào 邮票

Y P

▸ **stationery**

bàn gōng yòng pǐn 办公用品

BN GNG YNG PN

▸ **typing paper**

dǎ zì zhǐ 打字纸

D DS J

GENERAL INFORMATION

China's climate can be compared to that of the United States in that there are four seasons, a primarily temperate climate, and conditions that vary widely from region to region.

SEASONS

Spring

Chūn tiān　春天

CH(OO)N　T(EE)(E)N

Summer

Xià tiān　夏天

SH(EE)(ah)　T(EE)(E)N

Autumn

Qīu tìan　秋天

CH(EE)(OO)　T(EE)(E)N

Winter

Dōng tìan　冬天

D(O)NG　T(EE)(E)N

THE DAYS

Monday
Xīng qī yī   星期一

SH**ⓔⓔ**NG CH**ⓔⓔ** **ⓔⓔ**

Tuesday
Xīng qī èr   星期二

SH**ⓔⓔ**NG CH**ⓔⓔ** **⒜**R̲

Wednesday
Xìng qī sān   星期三

SH**ⓔⓔ**NG CH**ⓔⓔ** S**⒜**N

Thursday
Xīng qīsì   星期四

SH**ⓔⓔ**NG CH**ⓔⓔ**-S**ⓤⓤ**

Friday
Xìng qī wǔ   星期五

SH**ⓔⓔ**NG CH**ⓔⓔ** W**ⓞⓞ**

Saturday
xīng qī liù   星期六

SH**ⓔⓔ**NG CH**ⓔⓔ** L**ⓔⓔ**ⓤ

Sunday
Xīng qī tìan / rì   星期天 / 日

SH**ⓔⓔ**NG CH**ⓔⓔ** T**ⓔⓔ**ⓔN / R̲**ⓔⓔ**

THE MONTHS

January

Yī yuè   一月

ⒺⒺ Ⓨⓞⓞⓔ

February

Èr yuè   二月

ⓐⓗ<u>R</u> Ⓨⓞⓞⓔ

March

Sān yuè   三月

SⓐⓗN Ⓨⓞⓞⓔ

April

Sì yuè   四月

SⓊ Ⓨⓞⓞⓔ

May

Wǔ yuè   五月

Wⓞⓞ Ⓨⓞⓞⓔ

June

Liù yuè   六月

LⒺⒺⓞⓞ Ⓨⓞⓞⓔ

July

Qī yuè   七月

CHⒺⒺ Ⓨⓞⓞⓔ

August

Bā yuè   八月

Bⓐⓗ Ⓨⓞⓞⓔ

September

Jiǔ yuè   九月

JⒺⒺⓞⓞ Ⓨⓞⓞⓔ

October

Shí yuè   十月

SHⒺⒺ Ⓨⓞⓞⓔ

November

Shí yī yuè   十一月

SHⓊ ⒺⒺ Ⓨⓞⓞⓔ

December

Shí èr yuè   十二月

SHⓊ ⓐⓗ<u>R</u> Ⓨⓞⓞⓔ

COLORS

Black
Hēi sè   黑色
H⒜ S⒴

White
Bái sè   白色
B◌ S⒴

Blue
Lán sè   蓝色
L⒜N S⒴

Brown
Zōng sè   棕色
DS◌NG S⒴

Gray
Hūi sè   灰色
H◌◌⒜ S⒴

Gold
Jīn sè   金色
J◌N S⒴

Orange
Chéng sè   橙色
CH◌NG S⒴

Yellow
Huáng sè   黄色
H◌◌⒜NG S⒴

Red
Hóng sè   红色
H◌NG S⒴

Green
Lǜ sè   绿色
L◌ S⒴

Pink
Fěn hóng sè   粉红色
F◌N H◌NG S⒴

Purple
Zǐ sè   紫色
DS◌ S⒴

NUMBERS

0	1	2
líng 零	yī 一	èr 二
L(EE)NG	(EE)	(ah)R

3	4	5
sān 三	sì 四	wǔ 五
S(uh)N	S(ur)	W(oo)

6	7	8
lìu 六	qī 七	bā 八
L(EE)(oo)	CH(EE)	B(ah)

9	10	11
jiǔ 九	shī 十	shí yī 十一
J(EE)(oo)	SH(EE)	SH(ur)-(EE)

12	13	14
shí èr 十二	shí sān 十三	shí sì 十四
SH(EE)(ah)R	SH(EE)-S(ah)N	SH(ur)-S(uh)

15	16
shí wǔ 十五	shí lù 十六
SH(ur)-W(oo)	SH(ur)-L(oo)

17	18
shí qī 十七	shí bī 十八
SH(ur)-CH(EE)	SH(ur)-B(ah)

19

shí jiǔ 十九

SHⓊ-JⒺⓄⓄ

20

èr shí 二十

ⓐⓗℝ-SHⓊr

30

sān shí 三十

SⓐⓗN-SHⓊ

40

sì shí 四十

SⓊr-SHⓊ

50

wǔ shí 五十

WⓄⓄ-SHⓊ

60

liù shí 六十

LⒺⒺⓄⓄ-SHⓊr

70

qī shí 七十

CHⒺⒺ-SHⓊr

80

bā shí 八十

Bⓐⓗ-SHⓊ

90

jiǔ shí 九十

JⒺⒺⓄⓄ-SHⓊ

100

yì bāi 一百

ⒺⒺ-BⒾ

1,000

yì qiān 一千

ⒺⒺ-CHⒺⒺěN

1,000,000

yì baǐ wàn 一百万

ⒺⒺ-BⒾ WⓐⓗN

DICTIONARY

Each English entry is followed by the Pīnyīn spelling, Chinese characters, and then the EPLS Vowel Symbol System.

A

a lot hěn dou 很多 H⊛N D⊚

a, an yí yé gè 一个 ⊛ Y⊛-G⊛

able néng 能 N⊛NG

accident shì-gù 事故 SH⊚-G⊚

accommodation zhù sù 住宿 J⊚ S⊚

account zhàng hào 账号 J⊛NG H⊚

address dì zhǐ 地址 D⊛-J⊛

admission rù chǎng 入场 R⊚-CH⊛NG

afraid haì pà 害怕 H⊘ P⊛

after yǐ-hòu 以后 ⊛-H⊘

afternoon xià wǔ 下午 SH⊛⊛-W⊚

agency dài li 代理 D⊘-L⊛

air-conditioning kōngtiáo 空调 K⊙NG-T⊛⊛

aircraft fēi jì 飞机 F⊘ J⊚

airline háng kōng gōng-sī 航空公司 H⊛NG-K⊙NG G⊙NG-S⊚

airport fēijīchǎng 飞机场 F⊘-J⊛-CH⊛NG

aisle guòdào 过道 G⊚⊛-D⊚

all quánbù / dōu 全部 / 都 CH⓪⓪-Ⓝ-B⓪ / D⓪

almost jīhū 几乎 JⒺⒺ-H⓪⓪

alone dāndú 单独 DⓐN-D⓪

also yě 也 YⓐⓌ

always zǒng shì 总是 DSⓄNG-SHⒺ

ambulance jiù hù chē 救护车 JⒺⓌ-H⓪⓪ CHⓤ

American měi gúo rén 美国人 MⒶ-GⓌⓌ-BⓌ̲N

and hé 和 Hⓦ

another lìng yí gè 另一个 Lⓔ̲NG-ⒺⒺ-Gⓤ

anything rènhé dōngxi 任何东西 RⓌN-Hⓦ D⓪NG-SHⒺⒺ

apartment gōng yù 公寓 GⓄNG Yⓦ

appetizers kāi wèi cài 开胃菜 K① W④ TSⓏ

apple píngguǒ 苹果 PⒺNG-G⓪⓪

appointment yuē huì 预约 Y⓪⓪Ⓔ-H⓪⓪④

April sì yuè 四月 SⓏ-Y⓪⓪ⓔ

arrival dào dá 到达 Dⓦ Dⓐ

ashtray yān huī gāng 烟灰缸 YⓐN-H⓪⓪④ GⓐNG

aspirin ā sī pī lín 阿斯匹林 ⓐ-SⒺⒺ-PⒺⒺ-LⓔN

attention zhù yì 注意 J⓪⓪-Ⓔ

August bā yuè 八月 Rⓐ-Y⓪⓪ⓔ

author zuò zhě 作者 DS⓪⓪Ⓦ-JⓌ

automobile qì chē 汽车 CHⒺⒺ-CHⓤ

Autumn   qiū tiān   秋天   CH⓪⓪-T㊾㋐N

avenue   dà jiē   大街   D⓪-J㊾⓾

awful   zāo gāo de   糟糕的   TS⓪ⓦ G⓪ⓦ D⓾

B

baby   yīng'er   婴儿   Y㊾NG-ⓐⓗ<u>R</u>

babysitter   bǎo mǔ   保姆   B⓪ⓦ-M⓪⓪

bacon   xūnròu   熏肉   SH⓪⓪N-<u>R</u>⓪

bad   huài   坏   H⓪⓪⓪

bag   dài / dàizi   袋 / 袋子   D⓪ / D⓪-DS㊾

baggage   xínglǐ   行李   SH㊾NG-L㊾

baked   kǎo de   烤的   K⓪ⓦ D⓾

bakery   gāo diǎn diàn   糕点店   G⓪ⓦ-D㊾⓪N D㊾㋐N

banana   xiāng jiào   香蕉   SH㊾ⓐⓗNG-J㊾⓪

Band-Aid   chuàng kě tiē   创可贴
    CH⓪⓪ⓐNG K⓪ⓤ T㊾㋐

bank   yínháng   银行   Y⓪N-H⓪NG

barbershop   lǐfà diàn   理发店   L㊾-F⓪ D㊾⓪N

bartender   jiǔ bā zhāo dài   酒吧招待
    J㊾⓪ Bⓐⓗ J⓪ⓦ D⓪

bath   yùgāng   浴缸   Y⓪-GⓐⓗNG

bathing suit   yóuyǒngyī   游泳衣   Y⓪-Y⓪NG-㊾

bathroom (for baths)—yùshì   浴室   Y⓪-SH㊾

battery   diànchí   电池   D㊾⓪N-CH㊾

beach hǎitān 海滩 HⒾ-TⓐⱧN

beautiful měilì piàoliàng 美丽 / 漂亮
MⒶ-LⒺ PⒺⒺ-LⒺⒺNG

beauty shop fàláng 发廊 Fⓐ-LⓐNG

bed chuáng 床 CHⓄⓄⓐNG

beef niúròu 牛肉 NⒺⒺⓄ-BⓄ

beer píjiǔ 啤酒 PⒺ-JⒺⓄ

bellman xínglǐ yuán 行李员 SHⒺNG-LⒺ ⓄⓄⓐN

belt pídái 皮带 PⒺ-DⒾ

big dà 大 Dⓐ

bill zhàng dān 帐单 JⓐNG DⓐⱧN

black hēi sè 黑色 HⒶ Sⓐ

blanket tǎnzi 毯子 TⓐN-ZⓊ

blue lán 兰色 LⓐN

boat chuán 船 CHⓄⓄⓐN

book shū 书 SHⓄⓄ

bookstore shūdiàn 书店 SHⓄⓄ-DⒺⒺⓄN

border biānjiè 边界 BⒺⒺⒾN-JⒺⒺⓄ

boy nánhái 男孩 NⓐN-HⒾ

bracelet shǒuzhuó 手镯 SHⒾ-JⓄⓄⓐ

brakes shā chē 刹车 SHⓐⱧ-CHⓊ

bread miànbāo 面包 MⒺⒺⓐN-BⓄⓌ

breakfast zǎofàn 早饭 DSⓄⓌ-FⓐN

broiled　kǎo de　烤的　K⑩w D⑩h

brother (older)　gē ge　哥哥　G⑩h G⑩h

brother (younger)　dì di　弟弟　D⑥ G⑥

brown　zōngsè　棕色　DS⑩NG-S⑩

brush　shuāzi　刷子　SH⑩⑩ⓐh-DS⑪r

building　lóufáng / jiàn zhù wù　楼房／建筑物
　LⓄ-FⓐNG / JⓔⓔⓐN-J⑩⑩ Wⓐ

bus　qìchē　公共汽车　CH⑥-CH⑩h

bus station　qìchē zhàn　汽车站　CH⑥-CH⑩h Jⓐn

bus stop　qìchē zhàn　汽车站　CH⑥-CH⑩h Jⓐn

business　shēngyì　生意　SH⑩NG-ⓔ

butter　huángyóu　黄油　H⑩⑩ⓐNG-YⓄ

buy (I)　wǒ mǎi　我买　Wⓐ-Mⓘ

C

cab　chūzū qìchē　出租汽车　CH⑩⑩-DS⑩⑩ CH⑥-Jⓤh

call (I)　jiào　叫　Jⓔⓔⓐw

call　gěi... dǎdiànhuà　给　打电话
　Gⓐ Dⓐh-DⓔⓔⓐN-H⑩⑩ⓐ

camera　zhàoxiàngjī　照相机　Jⓐ-SHⓔⓔⓐNG-Jⓔ

candy　tángguǒ　糖果　Tⓐng-G⑩⑩ⓐ

car　qìchē　汽车　CH⑥-CH⑩h

carrot　hú luóbo　胡萝卜　H⑩⑩ L⑩⑩ⓐ-BⓄ

castle　chéng bǎo　城堡　CH⑩NG-Bⓐw

cathedral dà jiào táng 大教堂 DA JEE TONG

celebration qìng zhù 庆祝 CHONG-JOO

center zhōngxīn 中心 JONG-SHEEN

cereal màipiàn 麦片 MY-PEEAN

chair yǐzī 椅子 EE-DSEE

champagne xiāngbīnjiǔ 香槟酒
SHEEONG-BEEN-JEEOO

change (to) huàn qián 换钱 HOOAN CHEEAN

change (money) língqián 零钱 LONG-CHEEAN

cheap piányì 便宜 PEEAN-EE

check (restaurant bill) zhàngdān 帐单 JONG-DAN

cheers! gānbēi 干杯 GAN-BA

cheese nǎilào 奶酪 NY-LOW

chicken jī 鸡 EE

child xiǎohái 小孩 SHEEow-HY

chocolate qiǎokèlì 巧克力 CHEEow-KO-LEE

church jiàotáng 教堂 JEEow-TONG

cigar xuě jiā 雪茄 SHOOE-JEEah

cigarette xiāngyān 香烟 SHEEONG-YahN

city chéngshì 城市 CHONG-SHU

clean gānjìng 干净 GahN-JONG

close (to) kào jìn 靠近 KOW JON

closed guānmén 关门 GOOahN-MON

clothes yīfu 衣服 EE-F00

cocktail jīwěijiǔ 鸡尾酒 JEE-WA-JEE00

coffee kāfēi 咖啡 Kah-FA

cold (temperture) lěng 冷 LANG

comb shūzi 梳子 SH00-DSUr

come (I) wǒ lái 我来 Wah LI

company gōngsī 公司 GONG-SEE

computer diànnǎo 电脑 DEEN-Naw

concert yīnyuè huì 音乐会 EEN-Y00A H00A

condom bìyùntào 避孕套 BEE-Y00N-Taw

conference huìyì 会议 H00A-EE

conference room huìyìshì 会议室 H00A-EE-SHr

congratulations gōngxǐ 恭喜 GONG-SHEE

contraceptive bì yùn yào 避孕药 BEE Y00N Yaw

copy machine fù yìn jī 复印机 F00 YEEN JEE

    xerox fùyìn 复印 F00-EEN

corn yùmǐ 玉米 Y00-MEE

cough syrup zhǐ ke táng jiāng 止咳糖浆

    JUr K0U TANG JEEahNG

cover charge fú wù fèi 服务费 F00 W00 FA

crab páng xìe 螃蟹 PANG SHEEA

cream nǎiyóu 奶油 NI-YO

credit card xìnyòng kǎ 信用卡 SHEEN-YONG Kah

cup bēizi 杯子 BA-ZEE

customs hǎiguān 海关 HI-GOOahN

D

dance (I) tiǎo wǔ 跳舞 TEEOW WOO

dangerous wēixiǎn 危险 WA-SHEEeN

date (calender) rìqī 日期 BEE-CHEE

day tiān 天 TEEeN

December shí ' èr yuè 十二月 SHU eB YOOe

delicious hǎochī 好吃 How-CHEE

delighted kuài lè 快乐 KOOZ-Lw

dentist yáyī 牙医 Yar-EE

deodorant chúchòujì 除臭剂 CHOO-CHO JEE

department bùmén 部门 Be-MeN

departure chūfā 出发 CHOO-Fah

dessert tián diǎn 甜点 TEEeN-DEEeN

detour wānlù 弯路 Wah N-Lo

diabetic tángniàobìng 糖尿病 TaNG NEEw-BeNG

diarrhea lā dùzi 拉肚子 Lah-De-ZEE

dictionary zì diǎn 字典 ZEE-DEEeN

dinner wǎncān 晚餐 Wah N-TSah N

dining room cāntīng 餐厅 Kah N-TEENG

direction fāngxiàng 方向 Fah NG-CHEEeNG

dirty zāng 脏 DS@NG

disabled cán jí de 残疾的 TS@N-J㊐ D⓾

discount zhékòu 折扣 J㊐-K⓪

distance jùlì 距离 J⓰-L㊐

doctor yīshēng 医生 ㊐-SH⓾NG

document wénjiàn 文件 W⓪N-J㊐@N

dollar yuán 元 Y⓪⓪⑧N

down xià 下 SH㊐⓰

downtown shìzhōngxīn 市中心 SH㊐-J⓪NG-CH㊐N

drink (beverage) yǐn liào (n) 饮料 ㊐N-L㊐⓰

drugstore yàodiàn 药店 Y⓰-D㊐@N

dry cleaner gān xǐ diàn 干洗店
G@N SH㊐ D㊐@N

duck yāzi 鸭子 Y@-Z㊐

E

ear ěrduō 耳朵 @ᴿ-D⓪⓪@

ear drops ěrzhuì 耳坠 @ᴿ-J⓪⓪④

early zǎo 早 DS@

east dōng 东 D⓪NG

easy róngyì 容易 ᴿ⓪NG-㊐

eat (I) chī 吃 CH㊐

egg jīdàn 鸡蛋 J㊐-D@N

eggs (fried)   jiān jīdàn   煎鸡蛋   JEEN JEE-DON

eggs (scrambled)   chǎo jīdàn   炒鸡蛋
CHOW JEE-DON

electricity   diàn   电   DEEN

elevator   diàntī   电梯   DEEN-TEE

embassy   dàshǐguǎn   大使馆   DA-SHEE-GOON

emergency   jǐnjí qíngkuàng   紧急情况
JENG-JEE CHONG KOONG

English   yīngyǔ   英语   YENG-YOO

enough!   gòu le!   够了   GOL-LUH

entrance   jìnkǒu   入口   JEN-KO

envelope   xìnfēng   信封   SHEN-FONG

evening   wǎnshàng   晚上   WAN-SHONG

everything   yíqiè   一切   YEE-CHEE

excellent   fēicháng hǎo   非常好   FA-CHONG HOW

excuse me   láojià   劳驾   LOW-JEE

exit   chūkǒu   出口   CHOO-KO

expensive   guì   贵   GOO

eye   yǎnjīng   眼睛   YAN-JENG

eye drops   yǎnyàoshuǐ   眼药水   YAN-YOW-SHOO

F

face   liǎn   脸   LEEN

far   yuǎn   远   YOON

fare chē fèi 车费 CH⑩ F④

fast kuài 快 K⑩⦶

father rù kǒu 父亲 B⑩ K◎

fax, fax machine chuánzhēn jī 传真机
CH⑩⑩N-J⑩N J㊉

February èryuè 二月 ⑳B-Y⑩⑥

few shǎo 少 SH⑩

film (movie) diànyǐng 电影 D㊉⑥N-Y⑳NG

film jiāojuǎn 胶卷 J㊉⑩-J⑩⑩N

finger shǒuzhǐ 手指 SH⑩-J㊉

fire extinguisher miè huǒ qì 灭火器
M㊉⑥ H⑩⑩⑳ CH㊉

fire huǒ 火 H⑩⑩⑳

fire! zháo huǒ le! 着火了 J⑩ H⑩⑩⑳ L⑩

first dìyī 第一 D㊉-㊉

fish yú 鱼 Y⑩

flight hángbān 航班 H⑳NG-B⑳N

florist shop huā diàn 花店 H⑩⑩⑳ D㊉⑥N

flower huā 花 H⑩⑩⑳

food shíwù 食物 SH㊉-W⑩

foot jiǎo 脚 J㊉⑩

fork chāzi 叉子 CH⑳-Z㊉

french fries zhá shǔ tiáo 炸薯条
 J@ SH@ T@@

fresh xīnxiān 新鲜 SH@N-SH@N

Friday xīngqī wǔ 星期五 SH@NG-CH@ W@

fried jiān 煎 J@N

friend péngyǒu 朋友 P@NG-Y@

fruit shuǐguǒ 水果 SH@@-G@@

funny kě xiào 可笑 K@ SH@@

G

gas station jiāyóu zhàn 加油站 G@@-Y@ J@N

gasoline qìyóu 汽油 CH@-Y@

gate mén 门 M@N

gentleman shēng shì 绅士 SH@NG SH@

gift lǐwù 礼物 L@-W@

girl lǚ hái 女孩 L@-H@

glass (drinking) bōlī bēi 玻璃杯 B@-L@ B@

glasses (eye) yǎnjìng 眼镜 Y@N-J@NG

glove shǒu tào 手套 SH@-T@

go qù 去 CH@

gold jīn 金 J@N

golf gāo ěrtū 高尔夫 G@ @B-F@

golf course   gāo' ěrfū qiú chǎng   高尔夫球场
G(ow) (ah)R-F(oo) CH(ee)(o) CH(ah)NG

good   hǎo   好   H(ow)

good-bye   zàijiàn   再见   DS(i)-J(ee)(a)N

goose   é   鹅   (uh)

grape   pútao   葡萄   P(oo)-T(ow)

grateful   gǎn jī de   感激的   G(ah)N J(ee) D(uh)

gray   huīsè   灰色   H(oo)(a)-S(uh)

green   lǜ sè   绿色   L(ew) S(uh)

grocery store   zá huò diàn   杂货店
DS(ah)-H(oo)(o) D(ee)(a)N

group   tuántǐ   团体   T(oo)(ah)N-T(ee)

guide   dǎoyóu   导游   D(ow)-Y(o)

H

hair   tóufa   头发   T(o)-F(ah)

hairbrush   fàshuā   发刷   F(ah)-SH(oo)(ah)

haircut   lǐfà   理发   L(ee) F(ah)

ham   huǒtuǐ   火腿   H(oo)(ah)-T(oo)(a)

hamburger   hànbǎo bāo   汉堡包   H(ah)N-B(ow) B(ow)

hand   shǒu   手   SH(o)

happy   gāoxìng   高兴   G(ow)-SH(ah)NG

have (I)   yǒu   有   Y(o)

he   tā   他   T(ah)

head tóu 头 TO

headache tóuténg 头疼 TO-TONG

health club jiànshēn fáng 健身房 JEEN-SHUN FONG

heart condition xīn zàng bìng 心脏病 SHEEN DSONG BONG

heart xīnzàng 心脏 SHEEN JEONG

heat nuǎnqì 暖气 NOOAN-CHEE

hello nǐ hǎo 你好 NEE How

help! (emergency) jiù mìng 救命 JEE-MENG

here zhè' er 这儿 JOAR

holiday jiàqī 假期 JEE-CHEE

hospital yīyuàn 医院 EE-YOOAN

hot dog rè gǒu 热狗 RO GO

hotel lǚ guǎn 旅馆 LO-GOOAN

hour xiǎoshí 小时 SHEOW-SHO

how zěn me 怎么 DSON-Muh

hurry up! gǎnkuài 赶快 GAN-KOO

husband zhāng fū 丈夫 JANG FOO

I

I wǒ 我 WO

ice bīng 冰 BENG

ice cream bīng jī líng 冰激凌 BENG JEE-LONG

ice cubes bīng kuài   冰块   B(EE)NG K(oo)(Z)

ill bīngle   病了   B(EE)NG-L(uh)

important zhòngyào   重要   ZH(O)NG-Y(ow)

indigestion xiāohuà bù liáng   消化不良
   SH(EE)(ow) H(oo)(ah) B(o) L(EE)(ah)NG

information xìnxī   信息   SH(e)N-SH(EE)

inn xiǎo lǚ guǎn   小旅馆   SH(EE)(ow) L(U) G(oo)(ah)N

interpreter fānyì   翻译   F(ah)N-(EE)

J

jacket jiákè   夹克   J(EE)(ah)-K(uh)

jam guǒjiàng   果酱   G(oo)(ah)-J(EE)(ah)NG

January yīyuè   一月   (EE)-Y(oo)(é)

jewelry zhūbǎo   珠宝   J(oo)-B(ow)

jewelry store zhūbǎo diàn   珠宝店
   J(oo)-B(ow) D(EE)(ah)N

job gōngzuò   工作   G(O)NG-DS(oo)(oh)

juice guǒzhī   果汁   G(oo)(ah)-ZH(Ur)

July qīyuè   七月   CH(EE)-Y(oo)(é)

June liùyuè   六月   L(EE)(oo)-Y(oo)(é)

K

ketchup fānqié jiàng   番茄酱
   F(ah)NG-CH(EE)(é) J(EE)(ah)NG

key yàoshi   钥匙   Y(ow)-SH(Ur)

kiss (literally: "May I kiss you.")   qīn   亲   CHEEN

knife   dāozi   刀子   DOW-ZUr

know (I)   zhīdào   知道   JEE-DOW

L

ladies' restroom   lǔ xǐ shǒu jiān   女洗手间
　　LOO SHEE SHOO JEEEN

lady   lǔ shì   女士   LOW-SHU

lamb   yángròu   羊肉   YONG-ROU

language   yǔyán   语言   YOO-YAN

large   dà   大   DAa

late   wǎn   晚了   WAN

laundry   xǐyī diàn   洗衣店   SHEE-EE DEEAN

lawyer   lǔ shī   律师   LOW-SHUr

left (direction)   zuǒbiān   左边   DSOOah-BEEEN

leg   tuǐ   腿   TOOAy

lemon   níngméng   柠檬   NENG-MONG

less   shǎo   少   SHOW

letter   xìn   信   SHEEN

lettuce   shēng cài   生菜   SHUNG TSI

light   dēng   灯   DuhNG

like (I)   xǐhuān   喜欢   SHEE-HOOahN

lip   chún   唇   CHOON

lipstick   kǒuhóng   口红   KO-HONG

little (amount)   shǎo   少   SHOW

little (size)   xiǎo   小   SHEEOW

live (to)   huó   活   HOOah

lobster   lóngxiā   龙虾   LONG-SHEEah

long   cháng   长   CHONG

lost   mí lùle (adj)   迷路了   MEE LOO-Luh

love   ài   爱   I

luck   yùnqi   运气   YUN-CHEE

luggage   xínglǐ   行李   SHEENG-LEE

lunch   wǔfàn   午饭   WOO-FAN

M

maid   fú wú yuán   服务员   FOO WOO YOOAN

mail   yóujiàn   邮件   YO-JEEAN

makeup   huàzhuāng   化妆   HOOAh-JOOahNG

man   nánrén   男人   NAN-RON

manager   jīnglǐ   经理   JEENG LEE

map   dìtú   地图   DEE-TOO

March   sānyuè   三月   SAhN-YOOa

market   shìchǎng   市场   SHO-CHONG

match (light)   huǒchái   火柴   HOOah-CHI

May   wǔyuè   五月   WOO-YOOa

mayonnaise dànhuáng jiàng 蛋黄酱
D⓪N-H⓪⓪NG J⒠NG

meal fàn 饭 F⓪N

meat ròu 肉 R⓪

mechanic jìgōng 技工 J⒠-G⓪NG

meeting huì hì 会议 H⓪⓪⓪ H⓪⓪⓪ H⓪

mens' restroom nán cèsuǒ 男厕所
N⓪N S⓪-S⓪⓪⓪

menu càidān 菜单 TS⓪-D⓪N

message liú yán 留言 L⒠⓪-Y⓪N

milk niúnǎi 牛奶 N⒠⓪-N⓪

mineral water kuàngquán shuǐ 矿泉水
K⓪⓪⓪NG-CH⓪⓪⓪N SH⓪⓪⓪

minute fēnzhōng 分钟 F⓪N-J⓪NG

Miss xiǎojiě 小姐 SH⒠⓪-J⒠⓪

mistake cuòwù 错误 TS⓪⓪-W⓪

misunderstanding wùhuì 误会 W⓪-H⓪⓪⓪

moment piàn kè 片刻 P⒠⓪N K⓪

Monday xīng qī yī 星期一 CH⒠NG-CH⒠ ⒠

money qián 钱 CH⒠⓪N

month yuè 月 Y⓪⓪⓪

monument jìniànbēi 纪念碑 J⒠-N⒠⓪N-B⓪

more gèng duō 更多 G⓪NG D⓪⓪⓪

morning zǎochén 早晨 DS⓪-CH⓪N

mosque qīngzhēn sè 清真寺 CHⒺNG-JⓊN Sⓤ

mother mǔqīn 母亲 Mⓞⓞ-CHⒺN

mountain shān 山 SHⓐN

movies diànyǐng 电影 DⒺⓐN-YⓔNG

Mr. xiānsheng 先生 SHⒺⒺN-SHⓊNG

Mrs. fūrén 夫人 Fⓞⓞ-Bⓢ̲N

much (too) duō 多 Dⓞⓞⓐ

museum bówùguǎn 博物馆 Bⓞ-Wⓤ-GⓞⓞⓐN

mushrooms mógu 蘑菇 Mⓞ-Gⓞⓞ

music yīnyuè 音乐 ⒺN-Yⓞⓞⓔ

mustard jièmo 芥末 JⒺⓔ-MⓄ

N

nail polish zhǐjiā yóu 指甲油 JⒺ-JⒺⓐ

name míngzi 名字 MⓔNG-DSⒺ

napkin cān jīn zhǐ 餐巾纸 TSⓐN-JⒺN ZHⓢ

napkins (sanitary) wèi shēng jīn 卫生巾
 Wⓐ-SHⓊNG JⒺN

near jìn 近 JⓢN

neck bózi 脖子 BⓄ-ZⒺ

need (I) wǒ xūyào 我需要 Wⓐ SHⓞⓞ-Yⓐ

never yǒngbù 永不 YⓄNG-Bⓞ

newspaper bàozhǐ 报纸 Bⓐ-Jⓢ

news stand bàotān 报摊 Bⓐ-TⓐN

next time xià cì 下次 SHEE-TSE

night yèwǎn 夜晚 YE-WAN

nightclub yè zǒnghuì 夜总会 YE DSONG-HOO

no bú shì 不是 BOO SHE

no smoking qǐng wù xī yān 请勿吸烟
CHENG WOO SHEE YAN

noon zhōngwǔ 我 ZHONG-WOO

north běi 北 BA

notary gōng zhèng rén 公证人 GONG JEN BEN

November shíyīyuè 十一月 SHE-EE-YOO

now xiànzài 现在 SHEEN-DSO

number hàomǎ 号码 HOW-MA

nurse hùshi 护士 HOO-SHE

O

occupied bèi zhàn yòng de 被占用的
BA DSEN YONG De

ocean hǎiyáng 海洋 HI-YONG

October shíyuè 十月 SHE-YOO

officer guān yuán 官员 GOOAN-YOON

oil yóu 油 YO

omelet dànjiǎo 蛋饺 DEN-JEEN

one-way (traffic) dān xíng xiàn 单行线
DEN-SHENG CHEEN

onion yángcōng 洋葱 Y◉NG-TS◉NG

open (I) kāi 开 K①

opera gējù 歌剧 G◍-J◎

operator jīe xiàn yuán 接线员
J◉◉ SH◉◉N Y◎◉N

orange (color) júhóng sè 橘红色 J◎-H◉NG S◎

orange (fruit) chéng zī 橙子 CH◉NG-J◉

order (I) diǎncài 点菜 D◉◉N-TS②

original zhēng bǎn de 正版的 ZH◍NG B◉N D◍

owner yōng yǒu rén 拥有人 Y◉NG-Y◉-B◉N

oysters háo (or) mǔ lì 蚝／牡蛎
H◎ ／ M◎-L◉

P

package bāoguǒ 包裹 B◍-G◎◉

paid yǐ fù dè 已付的 ◉-F◎ D◍

pain tòng 痛 T◉NG

painting huìhuà 绘画 H◎◈-H◎◈

paper zhǐ 纸 J◉

parking lot tíng chē chǎng 停车场
T◉NG CH◍ CH◉NG

partner (business) huǒbàn 贸易伙伴 H◎◉-B◉N

party jùhuì 聚会 J◎-H◎◈

passenger chēng kè 乘客 CH◉NG-K◎

passport hùzhào 护照 HOO-JOW

pasta tóng xīn fěn 通心粉 TONG SHEEN FUN

pastry gāodiǎn 糕点 GOW-DEEEN

pen gāngbǐ 钢笔 GAHNG-BEE

pencil qiānbǐ 铅笔 CHEEEN-BEE

pepper hújiāo fěn 胡椒粉 HOO-JEEOW FUN

perfume xiāngshuǐ 香水 SHEEAHN-SHOOA

person rén 人 RUN

pharmacist yàojì shī 药剂师 YOW-JEE-SHUr

pharmacy yàofáng 药房 YOW-FONG

phone book diàn huà běn 电话本 DEEEN HOOA BUN

photo zhào piān 照片 ZHOW PEEEN

photographer shèyǐng shī 摄影师 SHOO-YEENG SHUr

pie (follow with name of filling) pài (or) xiànbǐng 馅饼 PY / CHEEN-BEENG

pillow zhěntou 枕头 ZHUN-TO

pink fěn hóng sè 粉红色 FUN HONG SUH

pizza bǐsà bǐng 比萨饼 BEE-SAH BEENG

plastic sù liào 塑料 SOO-LEEOW

plate pánzi 盘子 PAN-ZEE

please qǐng 请 CHENG

pleasure hěn gāo xìng 很高兴 H⓪N G⓪ SH⊕NG

police jǐngchá 警察 J⊕NG-CH⊛

police station gōngān jú 公安局
GⓄNG-CH⊛N J⓪

pork zhūròu 猪肉 J⓪-R⍉

porter fúwùyuán 服务员 F⊛ W⊛ Y⓪⊛N

post office yóujú 邮局 YⓄ-J⓪

postcard míngxìnpìan 明信片 M⊛N-SH⊕N-P⊛⊛N

potato tǔdòu 土豆 T⓪-DⓄ

pregnant huáiyùn 怀孕 H⓪Ⓘ-Y⊛N

prescription yàofāng 药方 Y⊛-F⊛NG

price jiàgé 价格 J⊕⊛-GⓄ

problem wèntí 问题 W⊛N-T⊕

profession zhíyè 职业 J⊕-Y⊛

public gōnggòngde 公共的 GⓄNG-GⓄNG

public telephone gōng yòng diàn huà 公用电话
GⓄNG YⓄNG D⊕⊛N H⓪⊛

purified chún huà de 纯化的 CH⊛N-H⓪⊛ D⊛

purple zǐ sè 紫色 DS⊕-S⊛

purse qiánbāo 钱包 CH⊕⊛N-B⍉

Q

quality zhìliàng 质量 J⊛-L⊕⊛NG

question wèntí 问题 W⊛N-T⊕

quickly kuài 快 K⃝⃝⃝

quiet ānjìng 安静 ⃝N-J⃝NG

quiet! (be) qǐng ānjìng 请安静 CH⃝NG ⃝N-J⃝NG

R

radio shōuyīnjī 收音机 SH⃝-Y⃝N-J⃝

railroad tiělù 铁路 T⃝⃝-L⃝

rain xià yǔ (v) SH⃝⃝ Y⃝ 下雨
　　yǔ (n) 雨 Y⃝

raincoat yǔyī 雨衣 Y⃝-Y⃝

ramp xié pō 斜坡 SH⃝⃝ P⃝

rare (cooked) nèn 嫩 N⃝N

razor blades dāopiàn 刀片 D⃝-P⃝⃝N

ready zhūn bèi hǎo le 准备好了
　　J⃝N B⃝ H⃝ L⃝

receipt fāpiào 发票 F⃝-P⃝⃝

recommend (to) tuījiàn 推荐 T⃝⃝-J⃝⃝N

red hóng sè 红色 H⃝NG S⃝

repeat! chóngfù 重复 CH⃝NG-F⃝

reservation yùdìng 预定 Y⃝-D⃝NG

restaurant fànguǎn 饭馆 F⃝N-G⃝⃝N

return huán 还 H⃝⃝N

rice (cooked) mǐfàn 米饭 M⃝-F⃝N

rich fù yù dè 富裕的 F⃝ Y⃝ D⃝

right (correct)   duì   对的   D⓪⓪Ⓘ

right (direction)   yòu   右   YⓄ

road   mǎlù   马路   Mⓐ-LⓄ

room   fángjiān   房间   FⓐNG-JⒺⒺⒺN

round trip   wǎng fǎn   往返   WⓐNG FⓐN

S

safe (hotel)   bǎo xiǎn xiāng   保险箱
    Bⓐ SHⒺⒺⒺN SHⒺⒺⓐNG

salad   sèlā   色拉   Sⓤ-Lⓐ

sale   mài   卖   MⒾ

salmon   guī yǔ   鲑鱼   G⓪⓪Ⓐ Yⓤ

salt   yán   盐   YⓐN

sandwich   sānmíngzhì   三明治   SⓐN-MⓔNG-JⒺ

Saturday   xīngqī liù   星期六   SHⒺⒺNG-CHⒺⒺ LⒺⓄ

scissors   jiǎndāo   剪刀   JⒺⒺⒺN-DⓄ

sculpture   diāosù   雕塑   DⒺⒺⓄ-Sⓤ PⓔN

seafood   hǎixiān   海鲜   HⒾ-SHⒺⒺⒺN

season   jìjié   季节   JⒺ-JⒺⓤ

seat   zuòwèi   坐位   DSⓄⓄⓤ-WⒶ

secretary   mìshū   秘书   MⒺ-SHⓄⓄ

section   jié   节 (or) zhāng (or)   JⒺⒺⒺ JⓐNG

September   jiǔyuè   九月   JⒺⓄⓄ-YⓄⓄⒺ

service   fúwù   服务   Fⓤ-Wⓤ

several hǎo jǐgè 好几个 HOW JEE-GE

shampoo xiāngbō 香波 SHEEONG-BO

sheets (bed) chuángdān 床单 CHOOONG-D@N

shirt chènshān 衬衫 CH@N-SH@N

shoe xié 鞋 SHEE@

shoe store xíediàn 鞋店 SHEE@-DEE@N

shopping center shāng chǎng 商场 SH@NG-CH@NG

shower línyù 淋浴 L@N-Y@

shrimp xiā 虾 SHEE@

sick bìngle 病了标志 B@NG-L@

sign (display) biāo zhì 标志 BEEOW J@

signature qiānmíng 签名 CHEE@N-M@NG

silence! ān jìng! 安静 @N-J@NG

single dānshēn 单身 D@N-SH@N

sir xiānshēng 先生 SHEE@N-SH@NG

sister jiěmèi 姐妹 J@@-M@

size dàxiǎo 大小 D@-SHEE@

skin pífū 皮肤 P@-F@

skirt qúnzi 裙子 CH@N-Z@

sleeve xiùzi 袖子 SH@@-DS@

slowly màn dè 慢地 M@N-D@

small xiǎo 小 SH@

smile (I)   wēixiào   微笑   WA-SHEE@w

smoke (I)   chōu yān   抽烟   CHO-Y@N

soap   féizào   肥皂   FA-Z@w

socks   wàzi   袜子   W@-ZEE

some   yìxiē   一些   Y@-SHEE@

something   yǒu xiē dōng xī   有些东西

    YO SHEE@ DONG SHEE

sometimes   yǒu shí hòu   有时候   YO-SH@ HO

soon   mǎshàng   马上   M@S-H@NG

sorry (I am)   duì bùqǐ   对不起   B@@ B@-CH@

soup   tāng   汤   T@NG

south   nán   南   N@N

souvenir   jìniànpǐn   纪念品   JEE-NEE@N-P@N

Spanish   xī bān yá rén   西班牙人

    SHEE B@N Y@ R@N

speciality   zhuān cháng   专长   J@@N CH@NG

speed   sùdù   速度   S@-D@

spoon   sháozi   勺子   SH@-DS@h

sport   yùndòng   运动   Y@-DONG

Spring (season)   chūn tiān   春天   CH@@N T@@N

stairs   lóutī   楼梯   LO-TEE

stamp   yóupiào   邮票   YO-P@@w

station   zhàn   站   J@N

steak niúpái 牛排 N⒠⒬-P⒮

steamed zhēng 蒸 J⒰NG

stop! tíng zhǐ 停止 T⒠NG J⒲

store shāngdiàn 商店 SH⒜NG-D⒠⒠N

storm bàofēngyǔ 暴风雨 B⒬-F⒰NG-Y⒬

straight ahead xiàng qián zǒu 向前走
SH⒠⒠NG CH⒠⒤N DS⒪

strawberry cǎo méi 草莓 TS⒪-M⒜

street jiē dào 街道 J⒠⒠ D⒬

string shéngzi 绳子 SH⒰NG-Z⒠

subway dìtiě 地铁 D⒠-T⒠⒠

sugar tàng 糖 T⒜NG

suit (clothes) xīzhuāng 西装 SH⒠-J⒬⒜NG

suitcase xiāngzi 箱子 SH⒠⒜NG-DS⒰

Summer xiàjì 夏季 SH⒠⒜-J⒠

sun taìyáng 太阳 T⒪-Y⒜NG

suntan lotion fáng shài shuāng 防晒霜
F⒜NG SH⒪ SH⒬⒜NG

Sunday xīngqītiān 星期天 SH⒠NG-CH⒠-T⒠⒠N

sunglasses mò jìng 墨镜 M⒪-J⒰NG

supermarket chāo shì 潮湿 CH⒪ SH⒠

surprise jīngyà 惊讶 J⒠NG-Y⒜

sweet tián 甜 T⒠⒠N

swim (I)   yóuyǒng   游泳   YO-YONG

swimming pool   yóuyǒng chí   游泳池
   YO-YONG CH⊕

synagogue   yóutàijiào huìtáng   犹太教会堂
   YO-Tⓘ-Jⓔⓔ⊕   Hⓞⓞⓐ-TⓐNG

T

table   zhuō zi   桌子   Jⓞⓞⓐh DSⓔⓔ

tampons   wèishēng shuān   卫生栓
   Wⓐ-SHⓤhNG SHⓞⓞⓐhN

tape (sticky)   jiāodài   胶带   Jⓔⓔⓐh-Dⓘ

tape recorder   lùyīnjī   录音机   Lⓞ-YⒺN-Jⓔⓔ

tax   shuì   税   SHⓞⓞⓐ

taxi   chūzū qìchē   出租汽车   CHⓞⓞ-DSⓞⓞ CHⓔ-CHⓤh

tea   chá   茶   CHⓐ

telegram   diànbào   电报   DⒺⓐN-Bⓞⓐ

telephone   diànhuà   电话   DⒺⓐN-Hⓞⓞⓐ

television   diànshì   电视   DⒺⓐN-SHⓞ

temperature   wēndù   温度   WⓤhN-Dⓞ

temple   sìyuàn (or) miào   寺院 / 庙
   Sⓔⓔ-YⓞⓞⓐN / MⒺⓐ

tennis   wǎngqiú   网球   WⓐNG-CHⒺⓞ

tennis court   wǎng quí chǎng   网球场
   WⓐhNG CHⓞⓞⓐ CHⓐNG

thank you   xièxie   谢谢   SHEE-SHEE

that   nà   那   NAH

the   zhè   这   JUH

theater (movie)   diàn yǐng yuàn   电影院
DEEN YENG YOON

there   nǎ lǐ   那里   NAH-LEE

they   tāmen   他们   TAH-MUN

this   zhè   这   JUH

thread   xiàn   线   SHEEN

throat   hóulóng   喉咙   HO-LONG

Thursday   xīngqī sì   星期四   SHENG-CHEE SEE

ticket   piào   票   PEEow

tie   lǐngdài   领带   LENG-DY

time   shíjiān   时间   SHE-JEEN

tip (gratuity)   xiǎofèi   消费   SHEEow-FAY

tire   lǔn tāi   轮胎   LOON-TY

tired   lèi   累   LAY

toast (bread)   kǎo miànbāo   烤面包
KOW MEEEN-BOW

tobacco   yāncǎo   烟草   YAHN-TSOW

today   jīntiān   今天   JEN TEEEN

toe   jiǎozhǐ   脚趾   JEEow-JUH

together   yìqǐ   一起   EE-CHEE

toilet   cèsuǒ   厕所   TS(ⓤ)-S(oo)(ⓐ)n

toilet paper weì shēng zhǐ   卫生纸   W(ⓐ)   SH(uh)NG   J(ⓢ)

tomato   fānqié   番茄   F(ah)N-CH(ee)(ⓔ)

tomorrow   míngtiān   明天   M(ⓔ)NG-T(ee)(ⓔ)N

toothache   yáténg   牙疼   Y(ⓐ)-T(ⓔ)NG

toothbrush   yáshuā   牙刷   Y(ⓐ)S-SH(oo)(ⓐ)h

toothpaste   yágāo   牙膏   Y(ⓐ)-G(ow)

toothpick   yáqiān   牙签   Y(ⓐ)-CH(ee)(ⓔ)N

tour   lǚxíng   旅行   L(ew)-SH(ⓔ)NG

tourist   yóu kè   游客   Y(ⓞ)   K(ⓔ)

tourist office   yóu kè bàn gōng shì   游客办公室

    Y(ⓞ)   K(ⓔ)   B(ⓐ)N   G(ⓞ)NG   SH(ⓔ)

towel   máojīn   毛巾   M(ow)-J(ee)N

train   huǒchē   火车   H(oo)(ah)-CH(uh)

travel agency   lǚxíng shè   旅行社

    L(ew)-SH(ⓔ)NG   SH(ⓔ)

traveler's check   lǚxíng zhīpiào   旅行支票

    L(ew)-SH(ⓔ)NG   J(ur)-P(ee)(ow)

trip   lǚxíng   旅行   L(ew)-SH(ⓔ)NG

trousers   kūzì   裤子   K(oo)DS

trout   zūn yú   鳟鱼   DS(oo)N   Y(ⓤ)

truth   zhēnlǐ   真理   J(uh)N-L(ee)

Tuesday   xīngqī èr   星期二   SH(ee)NG-CH(ee)   (ⓐ)R̰

turkey huǒjī 火鸡 H(oo)(ah)-J(EE)

U

umbrella yǔsǎn 雨伞 Y(oo)-S(AH)N

understand (to) lǐ jiě 理解 L(EE) J(EE)(UH)

underwear nèiyī 内衣 N(A)-(EE)

United States Měi Guó 美国 M(A)-G(oo)(UH)

university dàxué 大学 D(AH)-SH(oo)(UH)

up shàng 上 SH(AH)NG

urgent jǐn jí 紧急 J(EE)N J(EE)

V

vacant kòng xiánde 空闲的 K(O)NG SH(EE)(AH)N-D(uh)

vacation dù jià 度假 D(oo) J(EE)(AH)

valuable guì zhòng de 贵重的 G(oo)(A) J(O)NG D(uh)

value jiàzhí 价值 J(EE)(AH)-J(EE)

vanilla xiāng cǎo 香草 SH(EE)(AH)NG TS(OW)

veal xiǎo niú ròu 小牛肉 SH(EE)(OW) N(EE)(OO) B(O)

vegetables shūcài 蔬菜 SH(oo)-TS(I)

view jǐngsè 景色 J(EE)NG-S(UH)

vinegar cù 醋 TS(oo)

voyage hángxíng 航行 H(O)NG SH(EE)NG

W

wait! děng 等 D(UH)NG

waiter / waitress fúwùyuán 服务员
F⑩-W⑩-Y⑩⑯N

want (I) yào 要 Y⑯

wash (I) xǐ 洗 SH⑯

watch out! xiǎoxīn 小心 SH⑯⑯-SH⑯N

water shuǐ 水 SH⑩⑯

watermelon xī guā 西瓜 SH⑯ G⑩⑯

we wǒmen 我们 W⑯-M⑯N

weather tiāngì 天气 T⑯⑯N-G⑯

Wednesday xīng qī sān 星期三
SH⑯NG CH⑯ S⑯N

week xīng qī 星期 SH⑯NG-CH⑯

weekend zhōumò 周末 J⑥-M⑥

welcome huānyíng 欢迎 H⑩⑯N-Y⑯NG

well done (cooked) lǎo 老 L⑯

west xī 西 SH⑯

wheelchair lún yǐ 轮椅 L⑯N-⑯

when? shènme shíhòu 什么时候
SH⑯N-M⑯ SH⑥-H⑥

where nálǐ 哪里 N⑯-L⑯

which? nǎ gè 哪个 N⑯-G⑯

white bái 白 B⑥

who? shuí 谁 SH⑩⑯

why?   wèishénme   为什么   WⒶ-SHⒺN-MⓊh

wife   qīzǐ   妻子   CHⒺⒺ-ZⓊ

wind   fēng   风   FⓊNG

window   chuāng   窗   CHⓄⓄⒶNG

wine list   jiǔ dān   酒单   JⒺⒺⓄ   DⒺⒺⒶN

wine   pútào jiǔ   葡萄酒   PⓄ-TⒶⓌ   JⒺⒺⓄ

Winter   dōngjì   冬季   DⓄNG-JⒺⒺ

with   gen / he / yǔ (formal)   跟 / 和 / 与
GⒶN / HⓊh / YⓊⒺ

woman   nǚ rén   女人   NⒺⓌ   Ⓑ̱ⓊN

wonderful   taì haǒ le   太好了   TⓄ   HⓄⓌ   LⓊh

world   shìjiè   世界   SHⓊ-JⒺⒺⒺ

wrong   cuò-le   错了   TSⓄⓄⒶh   LⓊh

XYZ

year   nián   年   NⒺⒺⒶN

yellow   huáng sè   黄色   HⓄⓄⒶNG   SⒺ

yes   shì   是   SHⓊ   DⓊh

yesterday   zuótiān   昨天   DSⓄⓄⒶ-TⒺⒺⒶN

you   nǐ   你   NⒺⒺ

zipper   lāliàn   拉链   LⒶh-LⒺⒺⒶN

zoo   dòngwùyuán   动物园   DⓄNG-WⓊ-YⓄⓄⒶN

THANKS!

The nicest thing you can say to anyone in any language is "Thank you." Try some of these languages using the incredible Vowel Symbol System.

Spanish	French
GR@h'-S€€-@hS	M€R-S€€

German	Italian
D@hN-K@h	GR@h'T-S€€-€

Japanese	Chinese
D◯-M◯	SH€€€ SH€€€

Swedish	Portuguese
T@K	ⓄBREE-G@h-DO

Arabic	Greek
SHⓄⓄKR@hN	ⓔFH@hBREESTⓄ

Hebrew	Russian
TⓄD@h	SP@hSEEB@h

Swahili	Dutch
@hS@hNTⒶ	D@hNK ⓄⓄ

Tagalog	Hawaiian
S@hL@hM@hT	M@hH@hLⓄ

INDEX